More OF NEIL ZURCHER'S ONE TANK TRIPS

To Ginny!
Happy Travels!

11/29/97

Books by Neil Zurcher:

Neil Zurcher's Favorite One Tank Trips
More of Neil Zurcher's One Tank Trips

More OF NEIL ZURCHER'S ONE TANK TRIPS

GETAWAYS IN OHIO AND OVER THE EDGE

GRAY & COMPANY, PUBLISHERS
CLEVELAND

Gray & Company, Publishers
1588 East 40th Street
Cleveland, Ohio 44103-2302
(216) 431-2665
www.grayco.com

Library of Congress cataloging-in-publication data
Zurcher, Neil.
More of Neil Zurcher's favorite one tank trips : getaways in Ohio and over the edge / by Neil Zurcher.
Includes index.
1. Ohio—Guidebooks. 2. Ohio—Description and travel—Anecdotes. 3. Middle West—Guidebooks. 4. Middle Atlantic States—Guidebooks. 5.Southern States—Guidebooks. 6. Ontario—Guidebooks. I. Title.
F489.3.Z87 1997
917.7104'43—dc21   97-21158

This guide was prepared on the basis of the authors' best knowledge at the time of publication. However, because of constantly changing conditions beyond their control, the authors disclaim any responsibility for the accuracy and completeness of the information in this guide. Users of this guide are cautioned not to place undue reliance upon the validity of the information contained herein and to use this guide at their own risk.

ISBN 1-886228-17-5

Printed in the United States of America

10 9 8 7 6 5 4 3 2 1

With love,

To two people not yet old enough to have a driver's license:
my grandchildren, Allison and Bryan McCallister.
May they both someday have the adventures that I have had.
May they share the beauty I have seen.
And, may they always find something to smile about.

Contents

ONTARIO

Neil Zurcher and his BMW Isetta. *FOX 8 photo by Ali Ghanbari.*

Acknowledgments

I dislike the word "acknowledgment"; it sounds like you are being forced to recognize someone. That is not the case here. The fact is, without the following people there would be no "One Tank Trips," probably my career would have been much shorter, and there certainly would never have been a book, or a video, or a pamphlet about all those great places we have visited. So let's not call it acknowledgment. Instead, let me just say a very heartfelt thank-you to some very special people.

Virgil Dominic originated the idea of "One Tank Trips." Back in 1980, during the great gasoline shortage, he was news director of WJW-TV. He called me into his office one day to give me a new assignment: a weeklong series of stories about places that people could go that year, with gasoline in short supply, and do it on just one tank of gasoline. That was the beginning. Neither I nor Virgil ever expected the series to run more than just those five days. But it has now been on the air for more than eighteen years, chalking up the record as the longest-running local travel show in television history. Down through the years, Virgil has always been supportive of me and the show.

I am also very grateful to Bob Rowe, who succeeded Virgil as general manager of WJW-TV. He, too, was very supportive of the "One Tank Trips" series as well as my efforts to write books about the trips; he gave me much encouragement. He was also responsible for increasing the number of segments that are televised each week, from one to five. He was also responsible for letting me appear live on FOX 8's morning news twice a week to answer viewers' questions.

Mike Renda, who worked at WJW-TV back in the early 1980s, came back to take over as general manager from Bob Rowe. Mike, from the first day, has encouraged me to continue the series and also has been very supportive of my efforts to create this second book about "One Tank Trips."

Quite obviously, without all of this help and approval, I would probably still just be dreaming about some of the places I have visited, written about, and reported on.

Also, I can't forget the news directors down through the years: Virgil, Tony Ballew, Phyllis Quail, Grant Zalba, Kathy Williams, and my present boss, Greg Easterly. They rarely asked where I was going or what I was going to do, paying me the huge compliment of respecting my judgment when it came to "One Tank Trips."

There are many others: Margaret Daykin, our Specials Unit producer; Steve Golders, who presently edits the series each week; Richard "Zoom" Scott; Terry Trakas; Nancy O'Donnell; Kathy Smith; Tom Creter; Matt Rafferty; Phil Noftz; Maurice Sears. And I am sure I have forgotten some who also loaned me their talents to edit the "One Tank Trips."

Perhaps those I have been closest to all these years have been the WJW videographers who travel with me and use their cameras to capture what I see. They have done it in a magnificent way, and they have been wonderful traveling companions. From the beginning, Bill West, Peter Miller (now with WKYC-TV), Bill Wolfe, Jim Holloway, Roger Powell, Gary Korb, and Ralph Tarsitano have shared the road with me. They were later joined by Ted Pikturna, Cragg Eichman, Mark Saksa, Herb Thomas, Russ Herbruck, Cliff Adkins, Dave Hollis, Bob Wilkinson, Jim Pijor, Ron Mounts, Ron Strah, Greg Lockhart, and Ali Ghanbari. To each of them, and also to my good friends the late John "JP" Paustian and Dave Almond, thanks for the ride.

By now you may have perceived that it takes a large number of people to create a "One Tank Trip." There are also the talented graphics folks who work with me weekly, creating special openings and maps to go with the stories: Mark Neumayer, Kay Filla, and Christina Soehnlen. Kevin Salyer, Sam Lawson, and Nancy Wade in our promotion department help by publicizing the segments.

In many ways, I could probably list all the wonderful people I have had the pleasure of working with at WJW-TV FOX 8 down through the years. Each of them has had a part in creating this series.

Thanks also go to my daughters, Melissa Luttmann and Melody McCallister, and their husbands, Peter Luttmann and Ernie McCallister, for their help and advice on trips I have taken (and, to the girls, for suffering through many unofficial "One Tank Trips" when they were very young); my son, Craig, for all the trips he has helped on; and, finally, to my wife, Bonnie, who edits, checks, and rechecks manuscripts, lifts me up when I am down, and, most of all, loves me.

To all of you, thank you.

Neil Zurcher
Bay Village, Ohio

INTRODUCTION

To the Edge and Beyond

Over the years, since the beginning of "One Tank Trips," I have tried to take the show to the edge and beyond. What I mean is this: Why just stay in Ohio when looking for an interesting weekend getaway? Look at a map. If you live in Cleveland or elsewhere in Northeast Ohio, it's closer to drive to Erie, Pennsylvania, than to Columbus or Cincinnati, Ohio. The River City is a great place to visit, but it takes about five hours to reach the other end of the state. In that same time you could drive to Canada and visit a foreign country. You could be gambling at a casino in West Virginia in the same time it would take to drive to Toledo, Ohio. You could reach South Bend, Indiana, in the same time that it takes to drive to Dayton, Ohio. While Ohio is a great state in which to live, work, and play, we live in the middle of a great region, and many of the attractions in other states are no farther than some of the better known destinations within the borders of Ohio.

When Virgil Dominic, back in 1980, sent me on my first One Tank Trips for WJW-TV, I soon discovered that if I just visited places in northern Ohio, I would eventually run out of new things to see and do. So I convinced him to let me go "as far as a tank of gasoline would take me." I didn't tell him I was going to drive a car that got upwards of sixty miles per gallon. It allowed me to take in all of Ohio, to take our trips right to the edge of the state, and, finally, beyond, to West Virginia, Tennessee, Kentucky, Maryland, Indiana, Michigan, Canada, Pennsylvania and New York.

What we found on those journeys was a wealth of interesting places, things, and people. From the Pechin Cafeteria, in Dunbar, Pennsylvania (where you can still buy a three-course meal for just seventy-nine cents), to "seven acres of family fun" in a former canning factory just across the lake in Chatham, Ontario, in Canada. We drove deep into coal mines in Pennsylvania and found a submarine to sleep in in Michigan. A fantasy camp for race drivers in

Indiana gave me my first chance to take the wheel in a real high-speed race on an oval track. We rode a virtual-reality roller coaster in Toronto. We hummed along with people like Leonard Bernstein and John F. Kennedy, Jr,. when we visited the last American kazoo maker in Eden, New York. We found a store where you can outfit yourself in new clothes for ten dollars or less in Erie, Pennsylvania. We visited one of the greatest holiday outdoor light displays, just across the Ohio River at Ogelbay Park in Wheeling, West Virginia. For pure silliness, we discovered a "beer camp" in Kentucky, where beer drinkers can spend a weekend learning about and tasting hundreds of beers. Remember all the animated holiday displays that used to be found in Cleveland department stores? We found a place in Pennsylvania that brings all of those great Christmas windows back to life, and it's a free attraction. We paid a visit to the world's only tuba museum, near Lansing, Michigan. A jetboat took us up the New River through white water near Hawk's Nest, West Virginia. We stopped at a life-size replica of Christ's tomb in Kentucky, and climbed aboard a 100-foot-long tall ship for a cruise of Lake Michigan.

In short, we found that while it's great to take advantage of all the wonderful things that Ohio offers, you shouldn't hesitate to "go over the edge" to explore the other great attractions that are also just a One Tank Trip away in another state, or country.

To be sure, we have not forgotten Ohio. In this book you will find dozens of new, interesting, fun destinations in the Buckeye State. From a place where you can learn to drive a monster truck, to a real-life "Brigadoon" tucked away in the southern Ohio hills (a place where "only lovers are allowed"), to a spot where you can dive and see shipwrecks in Lake Erie. Our mission was to find and include things that often get left out of the tour books—places that may not be big enough to rate a review in national or statewide publications. Fun, interesting things to do that may fall through the cracks when it comes to letting the public know about them, such as solving the mystery of who puts those groups of three crosses along rural roads, or going behind prison walls as a tourist. If you find some of the places in this book and enjoy them as much as we did, then our mission has succeeded.

While I've made every effort to be sure that the information provided here is current and correct, no one can be sure that all of the places mentioned in this book will stay the same. Owners change, addresses and phone numbers change. If the trip is important to you, take the time to call ahead and be sure that everything is still as I said it was. It may save a lot of disappointment at the end of a journey.

Each time I start down a road on a new adventure, I keep thinking about an expression that was popular in the 1960s: "take time to smell the roses." As I drive along winding roads and find unexpected treasures along the way, I think of that expression and I slow my car to inhale the fragrance. Often, I stop to explore. My destination can wait for another day.

How to Use This Book

"How to use this book" seems like a really dumb statement. After all, you know how to pick a book off the shelf and open it up to the first page and, if you haven't accidentally turned it upside down, begin to read it. So, what does "How to use this book" mean?

For openers, I wanted to respond to some of the readers of my first book, *Neil Zurcher's Favorite One Tank Trips and Tales from the Road.* (Notice how I worked that plug in?) Some nice folks wrote us and said that they wanted some of the attractions grouped by themes. If they are interested in, say, flea markets, they don't want to have to search through every chapter to find all the flea markets. So, you will find two sections in this book. One offers traditional trips that cover a variety of things to see, do, and experience in a specific geographic area. The other groups unusual attractions thematically—by what activities they offer.

If you read my first book—no, I won't mention the title again—you may notice a couple of destinations that have been repeated in this book. That was done intentionally, either because they are destinations very near to one of the new trips, or because they were so appropriate for the new theme groupings.

But more than 95 percent of the listings in this sequel have never been collected in a book before. So, if you read the first book and enjoyed it, you'll find a whole lot more to enjoy here.

I hope you like this second book. If you have some things you would like to see in future books, drop me a line in care of the publisher. I'm always glad to hear from you, and I'll certainly consider any suggestions.

The destinations listed in this book have been chosen by me on the basis of my own experience and from letters and phone calls I have received from One Tank Trip viewers over the years. No one has paid a fee to be included here.

This book is not intended to be a technical reference work. You won't find maps or detailed directions. Instead, it is meant to encourage you to get out and sample some new places that might be fun, intriguing, and, hopefully, educational. Remember, half the fun of traveling is discovery. So, get out your map and plan your trip.

One last note: Always call first. Hours, prices, and even locations can change without warning. Especially if the destination is important to you, or is some distance away, be sure to call first.

SECTION I
If You Like . . .

Firelands Museum of Military History.

THRILLS

47 The Night of Flames

Their motors thundered and a high-flying cloud of dust spread over the county fairgrounds. Lucky Lott and his Hell Drivers had just completed the big finale: a jump by a man on a motorcycle, through a wall doused with gasoline and set ablaze, over the tops of three parked cars, and onto a ramp, where he landed safely.

All the way back to Henrietta Hill that night I dreamed it was me the adoring crowd had cheered and whistled for; I was that vision of a motorcyclist who came roaring around the racetrack, slid to a stop, and calmly stepped off his prone motorcycle, waving and acknowledging the homage being paid him.

The next day I rode my bicycle around and around our dusty parking lot, jumping it over small potholes and sliding to awkward, dusty stops to wave to an imaginary cheering crowd.

As the day went on, the pothole-jumping got boring, and a new plan began to develop inside my head. With my friend, Joe Cucco, I would do a real fire act with my bicycle!

That evening I invited Joe to join me in the backyard near the blackened ring on the ground where we burned our family store's rubbish each night. I had piled up several large, empty cardboard cartons. I also had a six-foot length of barn siding, my Flexible Flyer sled, an empty wooden pop case, and a two-gallon can of kerosene.

I explained my plan to Joe. We would saturate the empty cardboard cases and put them in the rubbish area. Half of the barn siding would serve as a short ramp to the top of the empty pop cases on one side of the fire ring; the Flexible Flyer would be the support for the remaining three feet of board that would be our escape ramp on the other side of the fire ring. Joe didn't like the use of the word "our." In fact he went so far as to tell me I was crazy and that he wouldn't have any part in such a stupid stunt. It was obvious that Joe had not heard the cheers at the fairgrounds. It also was obvious that if I was to duplicate the Hell Driver's bravery, I would now have to do it alone.

Though Joe wasn't interested in achieving immortality as the world's youngest fire-crashing bicycle daredevil, he was willing to help me do so. He would light the fire and stand by with a bucket of water, in case anything went wrong.

It was nearly 9:00 p.m. by the time we had sawed the board in two, made our rickety ramps, piled the cardboard boxes nearly twelve feet high, and soaked the pile with kerosene. I handed Joe a box of wooden matches. The air filled with the pungent odor of fuel oil as I strapped on a war surplus leather aviator's helmet I had bought for the occasion, pulled down the goggles, and nervously nodded to Joe that I was ready.

I rode my bicycle across the darkened lawn, ducking under my mother's clothesline, making a mental note to remember to duck again when I started my run. Near the highway I turned and faced the backyard. At that moment there was a giant *Whooshhh!* and flames shot fifty feet in the air as Joe scrambled back from the inferno he had touched off. Orange light filled the backyard, casting tall shadows on the back wall of our store. I could hear voices inside the store and knew that my parents would be coming to investigate any minute. My moment was now!

I leaned forward and started pumping. My legs were going like pistons, trying to get up enough speed to carry me through the fire and onto the back of the Flexible Flyer twenty feet on the other side of the firering.

I remembered to duck as I approached the clothesline, but not far enough. It caught the top of my helmet, ripping the goggles off my head. I barely managed to stay upright on the bicycle as I flashed by Joe, his mouth open in a giant "O." Somewhere in the darkness I could hear my mother yelling to my father, "Something's on fire in the backyard!"

I felt, more than saw, my bicycle hit the ramp to the top of the pop case. Suddenly I was surrounded by flames and sparks and heat, as my bike smashed into the crumbling tower of cardboard boxes, scattering them in every direction. The bicycle missed the Flexible Flyer, and the front wheel collapsed as it hit the ground five feet in front of the escape ramp. I flew off the seat headfirst, over the handlebars and onto the ground, where I slid through my mother's flower bed like a human bulldozer.

When I raised my head, I found myself staring at the startled face of the owner of that flower bed.

My mother, calming herself enough to make sure that I was still alive, ran to help my father put out the numerous fires created by the scattered, burning boxes.

Hearing the anger in my mother's voice as she scurried around the backyard stamping out burning bits of cardboard, and realizing that I was alive and well, Joe escaped on his bike and headed home, leaving me to face the music alone.

Aside from a few minor gravel burns on my forehead, belly, and knees, I walked away from my adventure intact. Sure, my parents were upset. My bicycle was impounded for a month. (It took me that long to earn the money to repair it.) And I was grounded for a month. But, truthfully, I didn't hear any of their words that night. All I could hear in my mind was the cheering of the crowd at the county fair. Lucky Lott's Hell Drivers' newest star had just made his first successful stunt run. Well, almost.

If you would like to try some daring feats on a One Tank Trip, consider these:

RACING FANTASY CAMP

If you are over sixteen years of age and have a valid driver's license, you can enroll in a two-hour introductory racing class here and actually drive a grand prix–sized racing car capable of speeds of over 120 miles per hour! And get this, you will actually take part in a real race with other students! The camp also offers in-depth driving training to professional race car drivers, for those who are very serious about auto racing. But for most of us, the beginner's course will more than get the heart pounding. You sit through a forty-five-minute safety lecture, where they explain the basics of race car driving. Then you suit up in coveralls, helmet, and a fire-proof hood, and climb into your racing car. An instructor leads you around the track a couple of times to let you get the feel of it, and then the flagman comes onto the track and starts the race. You go as fast as you feel comfortable going. Management claims never to have had a serious accident with student drivers. In my three-car race, I came in second, with a top speed of just over 80 miles per hour. (I chickened out on the curves.) Reservations are needed for both fantasy camp and in-depth training.

Fast Company, Inc. ☎ 317-653-2532
P.O. Box 151 • Greencastle, Indiana 46135
Location: Just a couple of miles from the famed Indianapolis Motor Speedway in the suburb of Greencastle.
Handicapped access: No hand controls in cars.

MONSTER TRUCK SCHOOL

Terminator III is a twelve-foot-high "monster truck" with a 1,500-horsepower motor. For about twenty-five dollars, you can take a ride in the truck with an experienced driver over a hill-studded course. As for the rides, there is no age limit, but they do recommend that if you have heart trouble, are pregnant, or have back or leg problems, this might not be the ride for you. It is very bumpy, and you will be required to wear a protective helmet and neck collar.

For the ultimate, you could spend a bit more and take a daylong course in how to drive the truck; you'd be allowed to run the course all by yourself and even crush some junk cars! The price of instruction is based on how serious a driver you want to become; it ranges from about $300 to $725.

Terminator III Racing Team, Inc. ☎ 419-627-6170
P.O. Box 160 • Huron, Ohio 44839
Location: In rural Huron County, south of Norwalk on Geiger Road, off Ohio Route 61. When you call for reservations, ask for map and directions.
Handicapped access: No.

INDOOR SKYDIVING

This attraction is truly unusual. (There is only one other like it in the U.S.) At the bottom of what appears to be an old grain silo is a large airplane motor and propeller blasting a wind of 150 miles per hour up to the top of the thirty-five-foot cylindrical shaft. Inside, customers wear parachute jumpsuits. A newcomer with no skydiving experience must first take a safety course. Then, instructors lead you into the silo and show you how to launch your body into the column of air. In seconds you are flying, up to thirty feet in the air, held there by the column of air. It is theoretically possible to stay up for hours, but most people stay up only for a few minutes. Be aware that there is some danger of falling if you disregard safety instructions. You will be required to sign a release form.

Flyaway Indoor Skydiving   ☎ 615-453-7777
519 North Parkway • Pigeon Forge, Tennessee 37863
Location: At entrance to Great Smoky Mountains National Park, near Gatlinburg, Tenn.
Handicapped access: Steps into chamber.

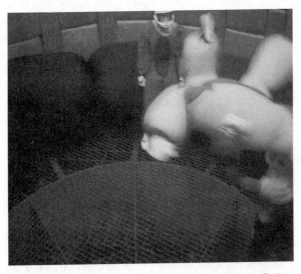

Flyaway Indoor Skydiving

PARASAIL OVER LAKE ERIE

Here is your chance to soar under a huge parachute towed behind a speedboat. It's relatively easy. You ride out into the bay on a speedboat equipped with a platform at its rear. You strap on a harness and are hooked to a huge parachute that trails out behind the boat. As the boat speeds up, a cable connecting the chute and the boat unwinds. The chute gently lifts you off the boat, and in seconds you are flying several hundred feet in the air behind the boat as it cuts through the water. On a clear day you can see the Canadian shoreline. As the ride ends and you are being winched back onto the boat, the crew gets a picture of you flying behind them so you can prove to your friends that you really did it.

North Coast Parasail   ☎ 419-627-2279
Oceana Midway Beach • Cedar Point
Sandusky, Ohio 44871
Location: Off public beach at Cedar Point Amusement Park, Sandusky, Ohio.
Handicapped access: Steps into boat.

WHITE WATER ON THE YOUGHEGHENY

This part of southwest Pennsylvania is the closest area to Ohio in which to experience true whitewater rafting. Available from early spring until late autumn, the route takes you through some beautiful parkland along the Youghegheny River. The rapids are rated as especially good for beginners but also offer challenges to experienced river runners. Boats, kayaks, and wet suits can be rented here, as well as at several places near Ohiopyle State Park. You can also rent bicycles to follow the Chesapeake and Ohio Canal Bicycle Path, which traces the edge of the river in this area.

Whitewater Adventurers   ☎ 412-329-8850
P.O. Box 31 • Ohiopyle, Pennsylvania 15470
Location: In southwest Pennsylvania, not far from Washington, Pa.
Handicapped access: Rough trail down to launching sites.

JETBOAT RIDE ON THE WORLD'S FASTEST RIVER

This is one of the most thrilling rides in Canada. Ride a jet-powered boat against the current, up the world's fastest-running river, the Niagara, through Devil's Hole Rapids, and into the giant whirlpool created at a bend in the river by the force of the water rushing downstream from Niagara Falls. You actually penetrate walls of water in the fast-moving jetboat. It's the only type of craft that the Canadian coast guard will certify as safe enough to make the trip. Riders must be over eight years old and must sign a release form. Bring along a change of clothes; this is a ride that will leave you absolutely soaked. The ride has been run for several years now without a serious accident.

Niagara Whirlpool Jetboat Ride　☎ 416-468-4800
Office at King George Inn
Box 1215 • Niagara-on-the-Lake, Ontario, Canada L0S 1J0
Location: Niagara-on-the-Lake is on the Canadian side of the falls, about 20 miles from the Rainbow Bridge that takes you from Niagara Falls, New York, to Niagara Falls, Canada.
Handicapped access: Steps into boat, rough ride.

Snake Hollow Adventures trail rides.

ATV TRAIL RIDES

This is a one-of-a-kind adventure. Mike Mouser operates the only ATV (all terrain vehicle) trail ride in the state. More than five thousand acres of the Wayne National Forest sprawl across Hocking and Athens counties; the forest service has staked out over seventy miles of trails just for off-road vehicles. Snake Hollow trail rides offer two levels of courses. A novice trail for beginners has hills that are not too steep and a trail that is fairly smooth. An advanced trail ride allows experienced riders to challenge what Mouser calls "aggressive trails," which turn out to be steep, rutted, and filled with rocks and roots and large (very large) mud holes that can nearly drown an ATV. He furnishes specially built ATVs that have automatic transmissions and electronic throttles. He also supplies the helmets, goggles, and gloves. It is strongly suggested that you wear shirts with long sleeves, long pants, and boots to protect your ankles. You will be given a short safety lesson before getting behind the wheel. The ride lasts four hours and costs about sixty dollars per person. There are discounted rates for groups. You will be required to sign a release form before joining the trail ride and must be age eighteen or older and have a valid driver's license to ride. Presently, the rides are held only on weekends, but Snake Hollow is trying to expand its schedule.

Snake Hollow Adventures   ☎ 800-582-3338
P.O. Box 731 • Logan, Ohio 43138
Location: They meet you at a trailhead in the national forest. When you call for reservations, they will give you directions. The forest is located near Logan, Ohio.
Handicapped access: No.

LEARN ROCK CLIMBING

Brian Still is an experienced rappeller and rock climber. He teaches both in the Hocking State Forest, near Logan, Ohio. Still claims that almost anyone can rappel down a cliff with a bit of training. Rock climbing, on the other hand, is considered to be one of the most physically challenging sports. While both activities use ropes and nylon straps, the equipment is different. For example, to climb rocks you need a pair of slightly small special shoes that have a sticky substance on the soles so you can get a better grip on rocks while climbing. Lessons are only offered by reservation. A four-hour course goes for about forty dollars. All the equipment needed is supplied; there is also equipment for sale to those that want to take up the sport.

Rempel's Grove   ☎ 614-385-5312
Hocking Hills Canoe Livery • 12789 State Route 664
Logan, Ohio 43138

ROLLER COASTERS

48 The Scream Machines!

I recently interviewed a man who had spent nine days riding a roller coaster at an amusement park. He did it to raise money for charity. When I asked him what he was going to do when he was finished, he replied, "Rest a couple of hours, then come back and ride it just for fun." Now, I like roller coasters. I have ridden them many times in my life. I might even ride three or four in a given summer. But this man—"Wild Bill" Cody, a radio personality from Cincinnati—had ridden the Screechin' Eagle at Americana Amusement Park in Middletown, Ohio, more than two thousand times in the course of nine days! That's a man who really likes roller coasters.

He's not alone; there are thousands just like him out there who spend their entire summer jetting around the world to spend a few minutes on a roller coaster. They are legend. They have also formed an organization: the American Coaster Enthusiasts, started in 1978 as a not-for-profit, all-volunteer club to foster and promote the conservation, appreciation, knowledge, and enjoyment of the art of the classic wooden roller coaster and the contemporary steel coaster.

Recently I met quite a few of these enthusiasts as I set out to do a series on "Scream Machines of the Midwest." Realizing that I was not a roller-coaster expert, I thought, who could better describe and point me toward the ultimate Scream Machines than members of the A.C.E.? I found out immediately that this is not a shy organization. Mention the words "roller coaster," coupled with the question, "Would you like to take a ride?" and volunteers come out of the woodwork. Some wonderful volunteers showed me the joy, and, sometimes, the pain, of many of the greatest coasters in the world, and they are all within a One Tank Trip of northern Ohio.

THE SCREECHIN' EAGLE

The Screechin' Eagle is one of two very classic wooden roller coasters still in existence in Ohio. Built in 1927, it is listed among the top twenty classic wooden roller coasters in the world by the American Coaster Enthusiasts. Riders say the recently refurbished coaster has lost none of its original appeal. Unlike other wooden coasters, its first hill is not the ultimate thrill. Rather, it's the short third hill that gives riders lots of "air time"—in other words, it literally throws them out of their seats. It is followed by several more quick, short hills that toss them into the air. The Screechin' Eagle is located at Americana Amusement Park near Middletown, Ohio. The park recently came under new management, which has spent considerable amounts of money upgrading the park and its fifty rides and attractions. No long lines here, and a ride on this classic roller coaster is worth the trip.

Americana Amusement Park   ☎ 800-486-3070 or 513-539-7339
5757 Middletown Road, Ohio Route 4 · Middletown, Ohio 45042
Season: May–September; closed on Mondays.
Location: On Ohio Route 4, between Cincinnati and Dayton, Ohio.
Handicapped Access: Yes, to some rides.

THE STEEL PHANTOM

Opened in 1996 as the "world's fastest roller coaster," this steel giant also offers the longest drop of any coaster in America—225 feet! At the loops, near the end of the ride, passengers experience a drop at more than three times the force of gravity as the coaster flies into the loops at eighty-five miles per hour. Members of A.C.E. had warned me that this is one roller coaster where you want to keep your eyes open. I rode it during a rain shower and made the mistake of closing my eyes. You get tossed around quite a bit when you don't see the loops coming and fail to brace yourself. The next time around, I kept my eyes open.

Kennywood is also home to Pittfall, the world's tallest free-fall ride. You sit in a chair with your legs dangling beneath you and are hauled up a tower, the equivalent of a twenty-five story building. When you least expect it, you are dropped straight down. A state-of-the-art magnetic braking system keeps you from becoming part of the sidewalk. It slows you gently, just before you reach the bottom. A great ride.

Kennywood has been named America's top traditional amusement park. It's a beautiful place, with lots of old-fashioned favorites as well as state-of-the-art rides and attractions.

Kennywood   ☎ 412-461-0500
4800 Kennywood Boulevard • West Mifflin, Pennsylvania 15122
Location: Kennywood is a suburb of Pittsburgh and is located southeast of downtown.
Handicapped access: Yes, to some rides.

Kennywood.

THE BIG DIPPER

The American Coaster Enthusiasts have placed The Big Dipper on their list of the top twenty classic roller coasters in the world. It is also the oldest continuously operating roller coaster in Ohio. Built in 1926, it has been thrilling coaster riders for generations. The coaster stretches for 2,680 feet and, according to A.C.E. members, is favored because each ride is different from the ride before, and there is "air time" at the crest of several of the hills. Geauga Lake, of course, is one of northern Ohio's major amusement parks and offers many other rides and attractions, including a steel coaster called the Mind Eraser that features three loops forward and then three loops backward, guaranteed to scramble your thoughts.

Geauga Lake Amusement Park   ☎ 440-562-7131
1060 Aurora Road • Aurora, Ohio 44202
Location: Aurora is just southeast of Cleveland.
Handicapped access: Yes, to some rides.

MAGNUM XL-200

The Magnum steel roller coaster seems to be a universal favorite with members of the American Coaster Enthusiasts. It was almost always mentioned as a first or second favorite wherever we went. Opened in 1989, it is nearly a mile long, with a 200-foot-high first hill that takes you on a dizzying plunge down several other hills, through tunnels and tight turns. After riding it several times, I understood why coaster fans enjoy it so much; it's a relatively smooth ride with lots of thrills and "air time." Cedar Point, of course, is the coaster champ, with, at last count, twelve major roller coasters. The park, with its many rides, historic hotel, and beach, is internationally known.

Cedar Point   ☎ 419-627-2350
Ohio Route 2 (One Causeway Dr.) • Sandusky, Ohio 44871
Location: On a peninsula in Sandusky Bay, west of Cleveland, Ohio.
Handicapped access: Yes, to some rides.

THE BLUE STREAK

This classic coaster was almost lost a couple of years ago when Conneaut Lake Park went into bankruptcy and closed. New owners rescued not only the park but also the wooden roller coaster, which was built in 1937. After extensive repairs, the Blue Streak reopened in the spring of 1997, just in time to celebrate its sixtieth birthday. The A.C.E. lists this coaster among the top twenty wooden roller coasters in operation. Park officials opened the coaster just for us on a spring day and let us ride it repeatedly to see just what was so wonderful about this old amusement-park attraction. Each seat on the coaster seems to offer a different ride, from a relatively smooth journey in the front seat to a rough-and-tumble flight in the rear. This was the only coaster that caused me to get a bit "green around the gills." I learned that the age of the ride, the height of the attraction, and the speed often have little to do with creating a thrill; that's more in the design. The Blue Streak is a fine example of a classic wooden roller coaster.

Conneaut Lake Park   ☎ 814-382-5115
12382 Center Street · Conneaut Lake, Pennsylvania 16316
Location: Conneaut Lake Park is just across the Ohio border in Pennsylvania, east of Pymatuning Lake.
Handicapped access: Yes, to some rides.

Cedar Point. *Courtesy Cedar Point.*

GAMBLING

49 Taking a Chance

If you like to gamble and the Ohio Lottery is just too tame for you, then consider traveling outside of Ohio to one of the nearby gambling casinos that are quickly surrounding us. You can now gamble legally in West Virginia, Indiana, Michigan, and Canada. Indiana offers riverboat gambling. The casino action in Michigan is confined to Native American reservations. West Virginia has put gambling machines in casinos at racetracks. Canada offers full-scale gambling casinos at both ends of Lake Erie. We visited several out-of-state gambling establishments and here is what we found:

THE CLOSEST (LEGAL) SLOT MACHINES TO NORTHEAST OHIO

This is the closest place to northern Ohio where you can legally play the slot machines. Mountaineer is a longtime thoroughbred racetrack that got into the gaming business a couple of years ago when the West Virginia legislature bowed to pressure and finally allowed slot machines to operate in the state at established race-tracks. Chester, West Virginia, is located just across the Ohio River from East Liverpool, Ohio. The day I visited, it appeared that more than half of the players were from the Cleveland-Akron-Canton area, all just down for an afternoon of gambling. For most of them the drive takes about forty-five to ninety minutes. The resort offers a small motel, a nine-hole golf course, tennis courts, a swimming pool, and a racetrack as well as the casino. They have more than 500 gambling machines in the casino. Machines offer slots, keno, poker, blackjack, and other electronic games. You don't get coins when you hit a winner; instead the machine gives you credit. When you finish playing, you touch a button to receive a printed credit slip for the amount of your winnings and take that to a cashier to be converted into cash. Mountaineer is open seven days a week.

Mountaineer Race Track and Resort   ☎ 800-804-0468 or 304-387-2400
WV State Route 2 • Chester, West Virginia 26034
Location: On State Route 2, across the Ohio River, about two miles south of East
Liverpool, Ohio.
Handicapped access: Yes.

DOG RACES AND MORE

Wheeling Downs greyhound racing has been popular with northern Ohioans for years. The dogs race year round, daily except Tuesdays. The recently added gambling casino offers more than 400 electronic gambling machines along with pari-mutuel betting. Unlike Mountaineer Resort, which is located in a rural area, Wheeling Downs is near downtown Wheeling, West Virginia, and offers a greater variety of tourist attractions, restaurants, and hotels. The gaming machines are open seven days a week.

Wheeling Downs   ☎ 304-232-5050
Wheeling Island • Wheeling, West Virginia 26003
Location: An island on the Ohio River in Wheeling, West Virginia.
Handicapped access: Yes.

LAS VEGAS IN ONTARIO

Casino Windsor, Ontario's first Las Vegas–style gambling facility, opened in May of 1994. Housed in a three-story building that was formerly an art museum, its fifty thousand square feet of space encompass roulette, blackjack, poker, and a host of other casino games, as well as over 1,700 slot machines. You must be at least nineteen years old to enter. All bets and winnings are in Canadian dollars. There is a currency-exchange facility in the building.

A riverboat, *The Northern Belle* casino is docked on the Detroit River in Windsor at the foot of McDougall Street; it has 820 slot machines and thirty-eight gaming tables. A currency exchange is also available there. A new casino, a third larger than the present building, is expected to open soon.

Casino Windsor   ☎ 519-258-7878
445 Riverside Drive, West • Windsor, Ontario, Canada N9A 5KA
Location: Downtown Windsor is located directly across Lake Huron from Detroit.
Handicapped access: Yes.

GAMBLING BY THE FALLS

This casino opened in late 1996 in what used to be a small amusement area just in front of the Rainbow Bridge to the United States. It, like the Windsor casino, is a temporary building; a new, permanent casino will be built within a few years. The facilities are much like Windsor's, as far as the gaming portion goes. Parking around Niagara Falls, already a problem in the summertime, is expected to be an even bigger problem for a while. It's recommended that you make use of parking lots on the edge of town that offer shuttle buses to the casino. Also, many hotels offer free shuttle-bus service. You must be nineteen to enter and play, but there are restaurants and a video room where children are permitted. One advantage to gambling at either Windsor or Niagara Falls is that Canada does not tax winnings. It's up to your conscience whether or not to tell Uncle Sam. The winnings are paid in Canadian funds.

As for the odds on your winning, while the casinos are quick to publicize big winners, longtime gamblers point out that odds are usually the best in towns where casinos have much competition for gamblers' dollars, like Las Vegas or Atlantic City. In Canada, West Virginia, and Michigan, local casinos have no competition.

Casino Niagara · ☎ 905-374-3598
5705 Falls Avenue · Niagara Falls, Ontario, Canada L2E 6T3
Location: Just off the Rainbow Bridge in Niagara Falls, Canada.
Handicapped access: Yes.

NATIVE AMERICAN CASINO

This is a small casino operated by Native Americans near Traverse Bay, Michigan. It has all the usual games and slot machines, and it is near a summer resort area featuring family activities.

Leelanau Sands Casino ☎ 800-962-4646 or 616-271-4104
Michigan State Route 1 · Sutton's Bay, Michigan 49682
Location: North of Traverse Bay, Michigan, at the edge of the bay.
Handicapped access: Yes.

MILITARY HISTORY

50 The Ballad of Rodger Young

Quick. Name the official song of the United States Army Infantry. No, it's not "The Caissons Go Rolling Along." It's "The Ballad of Rodger Young."

> Oh, they got no time for glory in the infantry,
> Oh, they got no time for praises loudly sung.
> But throughout the U.S. infantry shines the name,
> Shines the name of Rodger Young.

Who was Rodger Young and why did the infantry adopt a song about him? Young, born in Clyde, Ohio, enlisted in his local National Guard unit just prior to World War II. When war was declared, he was called to active service as a private. His life ended in an act of bravery on a faraway island when, during the battle of New Brittain in the Solomon Islands, his unit came up against stiff Japanese resistance.

A Japanese machine gun had the unit pinned down. Young, against the direct order of his lieutenant, crawled toward the bunker. Despite the fact that he was wounded several times before reaching the machine gun nest, he still managed to pull the pin from a hand grenade and to rise up and toss it into the bunker. As he did so, the machine gun fired directly in his face, killing him. Seconds later his grenade exploded, killing the Japanese and eliminating the threat to his platoon.

Song writer Frank Loesser, serving with the army at the time, was moved by Young's bravery to write the song. "The Ballad of Rodger Young" swept wartime America and was eventually adopted as the infantry's official song. Young was posthumously awarded the Congressional Medal of Honor, the nation's highest award for bravery. For a time, Rodger Young's name was one of the best known in America. But the war ended, and in peacetime Young and his heroic deed faded into history. Eventually, other wars called young Americans to battle, and new heroes and new legends were created.

On the thirtieth anniversary of his death, I was working as a reporter and became curious about this young private who had inspired a patriotic hit song. I went to his home town to see if any of his family was still around. Sadly, I found that most of them were gone. A few friends from the National Guard helped describe the boy from Clyde who had such bad vision that he had to wear eyeglasses in combat; who went to his platoon leader and asked to be demoted from sergeant to private because his hearing was getting bad and he feared that might put some of his men at risk. He was a man of rare principle and honor, an Ohioan with the instinctive courage to give up his life for his friends.

"What happened to the Medal of Honor given his family by Congress?" I asked. No one knew. They assumed it was in his parents' estate and that some cousin or friend might now have it.

I was also searching for a recording of the song "The Ballad of Rodger Young." Someone suggested that the Hayes Presidential Center in Fremont, home and burial place of President Rutherford B. Hayes, might have one in their collection.

The then-director of the presidential center, Watt Marchman, was most helpful. "Yes," he remembered, "there was a recording of the song made by the Clyde high school choir." He believed that there might be a copy of it in their archives. But a search of the stacks turned up nothing. Marchman refused to give up. He led me to a storage room in the museum and rummaged around on a high shelf until he found an old cardboard box full of pictures and documents. It was a box of miscellaneous papers and pictures given the museum by the Young family, but no one had yet gotten around to cataloguing its contents.

We started to dig through the box and within moments had uncovered not only a copy of the sheet music for "The Ballad of Rodger Young," autographed by Frank Loesser, but also a worn recording of the Clyde high school choir singing the song. We carried the box to a room with a playback unit, and as we listened to the song I was idly going through the rest of the things in the box. Suddenly I froze. There at the bottom of the box was a faded piece of blue ribbon with tiny white stars. I lifted several books off it and found myself staring at Rodger Young's Medal of Honor.

> Oh, they got no time for glory in the infantry,
> Oh, they got no time for praises loudly sung.
> But throughout the U.S. infantry shines the name,
> Shines the name of Rodger Young.

Following the war Rodger Young's remains were brought home to Clyde. He is buried in a quiet cemetery along U.S. 20 in the heart of the town where he grew to manhood.

For more on military history check out these other sites:

AMERICA'S FIRST PRESIDENTIAL LIBRARY

America's first presidential library is located at this center, the home and burial spot of President Hayes. The beautiful grounds of the estate, Spiegelgrove, are surrounded by gates that came from the White House in Washington, D.C. The museum tells the history of the nineteenth-century president and also has exhibits honoring many other U.S. presidents and featuring many themes from American social history. The nearby Hayes Mansion is much as he the former president left it; the home never left the Hayes family, and most of the furnishings are original. The museum library is considered one of the best in the country, when it comes to politics of the nineteenth century.

Rutherford B. Hayes Presidential Center   ☎ 800-998-7737
1337 Hayes Avenue • Fremont, Ohio 43420
Location: Fremont is in northwest Ohio, south of the Sandusky Bay area.
Handicapped access: Yes.

OHIO MILITARY HISTORY MUSEUM

· This small-town museum honors not only local veterans but also Congressional Medal of Honor winners from throughout the state. There is a good collection of uniforms and weapons from various wars in which Ohio soldiers have fought and a small library of reference books about the services.

Ohio Military History Museum   ☎ 330-832-5553
316 East Lincoln Way • Massillon, Ohio 44648
Location: In downtown Massillon, Ohio.
Handicapped access: Some steps.

Firelands Museum of Military History.

A HUGE COLLECTION OF MILITARY GEAR

This museum is not yet open but is expected to open in the spring of 1998 at the Huron County airport east of Norwalk, Ohio. It will include the private collection of war machines owned by Richard Rench, a former state representative and military collector. The collection includes a Vietnam-era M-60 tank, several smaller tanks that date back to World War II, two Huey helicopters from the Vietnam war, both in operating condition, and a host of other things ranging from a World War II flame-thrower to equipment from a Korean-War M.A.S.H. unit. All of it in operating condition. His plan is to offer rides in the tanks and helicopters, if not on a regular basis, at least during special events. It will be a one-of-a-kind museum.

The Firelands Museum of Military History ☎ 800-589-5880
Citizens National Bank Building, Suite 205 • 12 East Main Street
Norwalk, Ohio 44857
Location: Norwalk is in north central Ohio, near Milan and Sandusky.
Handicapped access: Unknown.

MUSEUM OF AMERICA'S TOP TANK GENERAL

This museum honoring famed World War II general George Patton is located at the army training facility at Fort Knox, Kentucky.
Visitors are welcome and admission is free. The exhibits inside the
building are mostly about Patton but also include captured tanks
from various wars. Outside, surrounding the building, are more
tanks from both the U.S. and foreign nations. There are also many
memorials to tank units that fought in the various wars.

Patton Museum ☎ 502-624-6350
4554 Fayette Avenue • Fort Knox, Kentucky 40121
Location: Just inside the gate at Fort Knox, Kentucky, a short distance from the
national gold repository, which you can not visit but can view from a distance.
Handicapped access: Yes.

WHERE GEORGE WASHINGTON LOST HIS FIRST BATTLE

The Father of Our Country, George Washington, fought—and
lost—his first battle here. That apparently bothered him so much
that after the revolution he came back and bought the land and kept
it in his family for years—probably to keep it from being made into
a memorial to his failure. The small wooden fort is now a national
battlefield park. Ranger-historians can tell you the story about how
the battle turned against Washington, and speculate on why he
ended up owning the battlefield. There is a small interpretive center
on the grounds. Admission is free.

Fort Necessity National Battlefield ☎ 412-329-5512
Farmington, Pennsylvania 15437
Location: On U.S. 40, in southwest Pennsylvania.
Handicapped access: Yes.

Fort Necessity. *Courtesy of National Park Service.*

SUBMARINE FOR RENT

If you have ever fantasized about spending a night on a real submarine, this is for you! The *U.S.S. Silversides* is a much-decorated World War II sub that is permanently docked next to a maritime museum in this Lake Michigan town. Families and groups can rent the sub by the night for reunions, meetings, even wedding rehearsals. But beware: there is no running water on the ship, and bathrooms are on the dock. You can spend the night in a bunk over a real torpedo (that, fortunately, has had the propellant and explosives removed).

U.S.S. Silversides Maritime Museum   ☎ 616-755-1230
346 Bluff • Muskegon, Michigan 49443
Location: Muskegon is located in the western part of lower Michigan.
Handicapped access: Ladder to interior of submarine.

INDIAN MOUNDS

51 More Travels with Craig

In my first book, *Neil Zurcher's Favorite One Tank Trips*, I detailed some of the problems my son, Craig, experienced while traveling with me over the years. Some readers wrote to me complaining that I had put my son in a bad light—had embarrassed him by telling the story of his becoming seasick while fishing. In truth, I've been the embarrassed one in a number of my adventures down through the years with my only son.

For example, when Craig was about eighteen months old I took him with me one evening to the local service station. I had shut off the car's ignition, but left the keys in the lock while I pumped gas into the car. Craig was at an age where he liked to stand behind the steering wheel and go "Vmmmm! Vmmmmmmmm!" I could see his head shaking excitedly as I filled the gas tank. As I stepped back to hang up the hose, I saw Craig turn and grab the sill of the car window, and in so doing, push down the door lock.

I desperately grabbed the door handle, trying to open the door before the lock closed, but it was too late. I ran around to the other side of the car and tried that door, remembering as I did that I always locked that door when Craig was riding with me.

Craig thought that it was a game. He was following me with his eyes, laughing, as I ran back and forth to the doors tugging at them with no success. As I came back to the driver's side, he had pressed his hands and mouth to the inside of the window, slobbering all over the glass.

"Craig!" I called to him. "Grab the silver thing there and pull it up."

I pointed to the pressed-down lock with no success. Craig continued to grin at me and slobber on the inside of the window.

By this time the service station attendant had come to the pump island to see what was going on.

"I think we have a door jimmy someplace," the attendant offered.

A minute later he tried to slide the slim piece of steel down the channel beside the window. The appearance of a stranger so close to the car had frightened Craig. He began to cry. I could only watch helplessly through the window as Craig's crying got louder and louder.

"I don't think these things work on Fords," the gas station attendant told me.

"What do I do now?" I asked, as Craig's cries rose to a new level.

"Well," the attendant said, shrugging his shoulders, "we can either break a window and reach in, or call the police."

The thought of breaking a window and showering broken glass over my already hysterical son wasn't very appealing, but neither was the embarrassment of having to call the law.

By now a small crowd had gathered around the car. One well-meaning man was tapping on the windshield, trying to calm Craig. A woman was shouting at him through the side window, "Don't worry baby! We'll get you out!"

All this confusion and noise just frightened Craig all the more, and his crying turned to red-faced screaming. A passing Westlake policeman, seeing the crowd gathered around my car, pulled into the station and joined the throng.

He offered to use a tire iron to crack the window, but I convinced him to try his door jimmy. He carefully slipped it into the channel by the window, fished around for a minute or two, and there was a click and the lock popped up. Craig had been rescued.

As Craig grew older we learned that he was less than impressed by some of the things we showed him. For example, we had traveled with a tour group to Alaska and had gotten up one morning at 3:00 a.m. to make a sixty-mile ride in an old school bus through mountain passes to gaze upon one of the truly magnificent sights in the Western world, Mount McKinley in Denali National Park. Guides told us that almost three-quarters of the people who make the trek never get to see the whole mountain because it is so high that it makes its own weather and is often sheathed in clouds. But this morning was special. The sun was shining, and, as we rounded a bend, we could see the mountain thirty miles ahead, bathed in sunshine, not a cloud in sight.

Even our guide, who drove the school bus along this route daily, whipped out a camera and joined us roadside as we clicked pictures of each other with the mountain at our back. I approached Craig with a microphone, asking him what he thought of Mount McKinley. He looked at the mountains surrounding us, and then at the towering peaks of Mount McKinley and said into the camera, "You see one mountain, you've seen them all."

Early pioneers and settlers in Ohio probably felt that if you had seen one prehistoric Indian mound, you had seen them all. The mystery behind these mounds didn't impress early farmers. In fact, they found the mounds to be a problem: they were too steep to plow. So the farmers started leveling them off in order to have level fields for their corn. It wasn't just the farmers who had no appreciation of this bit of ancient Ohio history. During World War I, the government leveled Mound City, near Chillicothe, and put barracks and a drill field over the site. Fortunately for all of us who enjoy history, some of the mounds have been preserved and are now protected from development.

MOUND OF MYSTERY

This is probably the most mysterious of Ohio's mounds. It is believed to have been built by Native Americans of the Adena culture around 700 B.C., though some say it may have been built as recently as 1300 A.D. The mound depicts what appears to be a huge snake about to devour an egg as it winds its way a quarter of a mile up a hilltop. It is not a burial mound, although burial mounds have been found nearby. No one is quite sure of the significance of the Serpent Mound. Perhaps it had religious significance; maybe it was used as some sort of calendar by early people. No writings about the mound have ever been found, nor any explanation of why it was built. An observation tower nearby provides a better view of the enormous serpent. The property is owned today by the Ohio Historical Society. The grounds are open weekends during April and May, and seven days a week from Memorial Day to Labor Day. There is an admission charge.

Serpent Mound State Memorial   ☎ 513-587-2796
3850 Ohio Route 73 · Peebles, Ohio 45660
Location: Near Hillsboro, Ohio, about an hour east of Cincinnati.
Handicapped Access: Yes.

Serpent Mound. *Courtesy of Ohio Historical Society.*

MOUND CITY

Twenty-three mounds spread across thirteen acres, surrounded by a low earthen wall, are all that remains of a once larger site. Many of these were burial mounds. Researchers have no real idea just what the other mounds were meant to signify, or why they were built at this location. In recent years, at least one of the mounds was opened so tourists could look inside. However, in response to objections by Native American groups, who felt that the open mound showed disrespect for a grave, the National Park Service closed the mound and instead displays pictures of it in the nearby interpretive center.

Mound City, Hopewell Culture National Hist. Park   ☎ 614-774-1125
16062 State Route 104 · Chillicothe, Ohio 45601
Location: Chillicothe is south of Columbus, Ohio.
Handicapped access: Yes.

PREHISTORIC MOUNDS AND FLINT

The Newark Earthworks is another mystery for residents of modern-day central Ohio. The Earthworks, an earthen wall, stretched for miles. No one is sure whether it was meant for defense or, perhaps, some religious rite. One thing is for sure: the wall was built by prehistoric Hopewell people sometime between 100 B.C. and 400 A.D. Some bodies have been found in parts of the wall and in mounds nearby. Also nearby is Flint Ridge State Memorial, where early Native Americans came to get the flint they used for knives and arrow points. Many of the flint outcroppings are still visible, as are quarry holes dug by prehistoric people searching for the flint. Interpretive centers at both memorials display artifacts found at the sites, and guides help give a better understanding of one of Ohio's most lasting mysteries. The earthworks are open year round.

The Newark Earthworks/Moundbuilders State Memorial
99 Cooper Avenue • Newark, Ohio 43055
Location: Newark, Ohio, is located east of Columbus in central Ohio.
Handicapped access: Yes.

Newark Mound. *Courtesy of National Park Service.*

HOLIDAY LIGHTS

52 A Million or More Lights

The current craze of holiday light festivals may have started nearby at Niagara Falls in the 1980s, when the Canadian and U.S. sides first began lighting up for Christmas. The display was so popular that it has been repeated every year since. Now, more than a million lights illuminate both sides of Niagara Falls from November until mid-January. The lights, which can be seen from both sides of the river, are accompanied by animations and live shows—also on both sides of the international line. Many cities have copied the idea, the the original is still one of the best.

Niagara Falls Festival of the Lights   ☎ 716-285-2400
Niagara Falls, NY 14303
Location: The zoo is in the northern part of downtown Cincinnati.
Handicapped access: Yes.

OGELBAY PARK

Ogelbay Park got into the holiday light festival about the same time as Niagara Falls, and the mountaintop display here has continued to grow each year. It now tops over one million colored lights and displays, and turns the Mountain State night into a fantasyland of color. The headlights from the hundreds of thousands of automobiles that drive up and down the mountain only add to this wintertime tourist attraction, which draws visitors from several states.

While there is no admission charge to drive through the park and see the lights, donations are taken to help enlarge the collection. In addition to the lights, there are tours of the Ogelbay Mansion (at the park entrance) and an enormous model train display at the zoo building.

Ogelbay Park was once the summer home of the Ogelbay family of Cleveland. On the owner's death, it was given to the city of Wheeling for use as a city park. Today the mountaintop resort has a large lodge, cabins, three golf courses, bridle trails, fishing, and a host of other activities that make it one of the major tourist attractions of West Virginia.

Ogelbay Park   ☎ 800-624-6988
Wheeling, West Virginia 26003
Location: Just across the Ohio River and south of downtown Wheeling, West Virginia.
Handicapped access: Yes.

RUDD'S CHRISTMAS FARM

From the day after Thanksgiving to New Year's Day, this valley experiences a holiday miracle. Members of the Rudd family, who live in a log cabin at the end of Cassel Run, in a small valley in southern Ohio, put up hundreds of thousands of lights and homemade displays until their valley is filled from hill to hill with light. Then they invite everybody to stop by and ogle. There's no charge; it's just their gift to humankind. Even though the Rudd farm is located in a remote, sparsely populated rural area, people come. They come in buses and cars, usually jamming the roads on the weekends. All the work of hanging and maintaining the lights is done by the Rudd family. In fact, Mr. Rudd, a retired janitor, has even been known to borrow money at Christmas in order to keep the lights on.

Rudd's Christmas Farm   ☎ 513-544-3500
1205 Cassel Run Road • Blue Creek, Ohio 45616
Location: West of Portsmouth, Ohio.
Handicapped access: Steps to some of the displays.

INTERNATIONAL FESTIVAL OF LIGHTS

This is one of the newest of the light festivals. It started in the early 1990s and has grown by leaps and bounds each year. It now claims upwards of a million lights spread across this city made famous by cereal kings Post and Kellogg. In fact you'll probably see Tony the Tiger and Snap, Crackle, and Pop outlined in lights in front of the Kellogg factory. There are walking tours of the city at night, and a headquarters where Santa Claus is waiting to meet the kids. Plenty of hot chocolate and holiday songs. If the cereal companies continue to back this festival, it may become one of the biggest in the nation.

International Festival of Lights   ☎ 800-397-2240
Battle Creek, Michigan
Location: Battle Creek is in central lower Michigan.
Handicapped access: Yes.

CINCINNATI ZOO AND BOTANICAL GARDENS

USA Today tagged the Cincinnati Zoo Holiday Light Festival as one of the "ten best in the nation." I won't argue. It's a true fairyland at night when there's snow on the ground. Besides hundreds of thousands of lights, there are many other attractions, from an ice show to a camel ride. Trains run all over the park; big trains and little trains. Even the zoo's maternity ward is open; there you can see live baby monkeys, lions, and whatever else happens to be born during the Christmas season.

Cincinnati Zoo and Botanical Gardens   ☎ 513-281-4700
300 Vine Street • Cincinnati, Ohio 45220
Location: The zoo is in the northern part of downtown Cincinnati.
Handicapped access: Yes.

Cincinnati Zoo Holiday Light Festival. *Courtesy of Cincinnati Zoo.*

CAVERNS

53 The Caviest Cave in the United States

The "Caviest Cave in the United States": that's what some cave fanciers have tagged Seneca Caverns, near Bellevue, Ohio. That's because although the caves have been a tourist attraction for a half century or more, they have been left much the way they were found or first excavated. In other words, there are no smooth, measured steps down to each level; just a path and sometimes narrow passageways and uneven rocks to climb on. There are several levels to the caverns, and more than half of the caverns are yet unexplored. If you like your caves to look like caves, this is the one for you. But it's not for everyone, especially if you have trouble walking and climbing or don't like tight passageways.

The Seneca Caverns complex was discovered in 1872 by two boys who fell into part of it while searching for their dog. It has seven levels and runs to 110 feet deep; the largest room is 250 feet long. A crystal-clear spring is located on the lowest level. Bring a sweater or coat—the temperature inside the caverns is always 54 degrees. This cave, they say, is unusual because it was formed from a crack in the earth. Owner Dick Bell says his father commercialized the caverns and first opened them to tourists in the early 1930s, during the Depression. (His father was an attorney and sometimes would let clients work off their bills by helping clean mud out of cavern passages.) When we have an especially wet spring or summer, the lower levels of the caverns are often filled with water.

Seneca Caverns ☎ 419-483-6711
Bellevue, Ohio 44811
Location: Actually near the small town of Flat Rock, south of Bellevue, Ohio.
Handicapped access: No.

OLENTANGY INDIAN CAVERNS

These caverns, formed by an underground river, have been explored to a level of 150 feet down from the surface. There are several levels, and some of the passages are believed to lead to the Olentangy River a half mile away. The caverns were first used by the Wyandot Indians as a hiding place and for tribal ceremonies. The great Chief Leatherlips was killed by his own people at the entrance to the caverns. I like these caverns because they are roomy, reasonably easy to tour, and have smooth passageways and steps.

Olentangy Indian Caverns   ☎ 614-548-7917
1779 Home Road · Delaware, Ohio 43015
Location: Just north of Columbus, near Delaware, Ohio.
Handicapped access: No, many steps.

THE LARGEST CAVE IN PENNSYLVANIA

This is the largest cave in Pennsylvania and has miles of passages. Although discovered and explored in the 1700s, it was not developed into a tourist attraction until 1962. It offers both guided tours and self-guided tours. Rappelling and caving lessons are also available. Open daily from May to October; weekends only during March, April, and November.

Laurel Caverns is not far from Fort Necessity, site of the only battle lost by George Washington.

Laurel Caverns   ☎ 412-438-3003
R.D. #1, Box 10 · Farmington, Pennsylvania 15437
Location: Near U.S. Route 40, east of Uniontown, Pennsylvania.
Handicapped access: Steps into cave.

THE BIGGEST CAVE SYSTEM IN OHIO

Ohio Caverns are promoted as the largest and most beautiful cave system in Ohio. Their crystal-white stalactite and stalagmite formations are still developing. The temperature of the cave, like most caves, is a constant 54 degrees, so bring a coat or sweater. The tour route through the caverns is level, which makes it much easier for people who do not like climbing and uneven floors.

Ohio Caverns   ☎ 937-465-4017
2210 Ohio Route 245 East · West Liberty, Ohio 43357
Location: In west central Ohio.
Handicapped access: No, steps to cave.

"Cavern of the Gods," Ohio Caverns. *Courtesy of Ohio Caverns.*

SORT OF A CAVE

Okay, this isn't a real cave. But if you have some little ones who are nervous about going into a real cave, you might want to start out at the Erie (Pennsylvania) Children's Museum. Among its many hands-on attractions is a realistic cave, where the kids can find prehistoric writings on the wall and learn how gas is created inside the earth. There are also a lot of other fun things for the kids to do here. A must-see if you are in Erie.

Experience Children's Museum   ☎ 814-453-3743
420 French Street · Erie, Pennsylvania 16507
Location: In downtown Erie, Pennsylvania.
Handicapped access: Yes.

ANIMALS

54 Talk and Play with the Animals

Was Dr. Doolittle a big hit with your family? If so, there's a place in Ohio's Amish country you should know about, where you can really get up close and personal with wild animals.

Some of the Amish deal in exotic animals, raising and selling them to animal preserves, hunting preserves, or for their meat. But down in Holmes County, one Amish family noticed how many tourists would slow down when passing their farm to gawk at the llamas, water buffalo, and other wild creatures waiting in their pastures until the next exotic animal auction. This past autumn, idea became reality, and Rolling Ridge Ranch was born.

Here you have several options.

You can pay your admission and drive your car through a trail on the 100-acre farm. The trail passes through forests and pastures and offers a very close look at the dozens of exotic animals that now call this place home: bull elk, tiny pot-bellied pigs, African cattle with twelve-foot-wide horns, seven-foot-tall ostriches, zebras, mountain goats, and even water buffalo.

If you really want to get up close and personal, opt for either the horse-drawn wagon ride or the horse-drawn carriage ride through the preserve. The wagon is usually driven by the person who feeds the animals, and as soon as they see the wagon, those animals come running. It is a bit disconcerting to be far back in a forest on a hillside road and suddenly see an eight-foot-tall bull elk plunging through the underbrush headed straight for you. But all he wants is his share of the grain that is on board the wagon. Goats even try to get on the wagon with you. Some of the animals, like the zebras, can get a bit aggressive when you run out of feed to give them; they think you might be hiding some in the wagon. Much the same thing happens on the carriage ride. If you have the white feed buckets, all the animals come running and try to join you in the carriage if you don't offer the grain fast enough. The wagon or carriage ride may not be suitable for small or easily frightened children.

At the conclusion of the ride, you are invited to the gift shop, where T-shirts and the usual souvenirs are on sale. There is also a petting zoo, where baby pigs, ducks, and even miniature donkeys are just waiting for a youngster with some food.

Rolling Ridge Ranch   ☎ 330-893-3777
3961 County Road 168 • Millersburg, Ohio 44654
Ranch is open for tours from spring until late autumn.
Location: Ranch is actually located just north of town of Berlin, which is east of Millersburg. Watch for signs.
Handicapped access: Yes, in car or van.

AN OHIO REFUGE FOR ENDANGERED SPECIES

This is going to be one of Ohio's major tourist attractions. Only open a few years, it is already attracting thousands from around the nation. It is a refuge where endangered exotic animals from all over the world are allowed to run free on seventeen square miles of reclaimed strip-mined land. Over two hundred different animals, some already extinct in their native lands, are housed here. (Animals from tropical areas are sheltered in barns for the winter months.)

Visitors are allowed inside the compound only on board special buses with guides. Touching or feeding the animals is not allowed. As the animals roam free, there is no guarantee what you will see. When the animals are near the roads you can get an up-close look. If they choose to hide in nearby groves of trees you get only a ride. However, many of the animals here were born in captivity and are accustomed to people, if not downright curious; it's a rare visit when you don't see several of the endangered species.

Among the animals in the compound are giraffes, white rhinos, eland, camels, and some rare Mongolian ponies. Management hopes to add some elephants this year. The animals chosen are of species that are rare or endangered, and the purpose is to keep the breed going by offering them shelter here in Ohio at the Wilds.

There is an admission charge. The Wilds is open from May to October.

The Wilds   ☎ 614-638-5030 or 614-439-1472
14000 International Road • Cambridge, Ohio 43732
Location: South of Cambridge, Ohio. Call for map and directions.
Handicapped access: Yes.

The Wilds. *Courtesy of The Wilds.*

AUTOMOBILE SAFARI

If you'd enjoy being slobbered on by a llama or a camel, this is the place for you. As you drive your car through this compound, be prepared to be very popular if the animals spot you with one of the little white feed buckets. Your windshield will probably be licked clean by an eland or a zebra. Also, if you have the window down far enough, a deer with halitosis may give you a big wet kiss while trying to steal the entire bucket of food.

Besides the drive-through portion of the park, you can also visit a walk-through petting zoo, see some baby animals, and get a pony or camel ride.

African Safari Wildlife Park   ☎ 800-521-2660 or 419-732-3606
267 Lightner Road • Port Clinton, Ohio 43452
Location: Just east of Port Clinton, Ohio.
Handicapped access: Yes.

ROMANCE

55 A.K.A. Cupid

During my twoscore years as a journalist, I have been called upon to do some rather silly things, like taking my clothes off when visiting a nudist colony, or climbing a rope down the outside of our television station.

One of the silliest was the time in 1995 when we decided to run a contest along with my weeklong series about romantic getaway places. The promotion department wanted to dress me up as Cupid to plug the contest at the end of each night's segment. I immediately balked at the thought of running around in public wearing nothing but a diaper and carrying a bow and arrow.

"Wear anything you like," said Kevin Salyer of our Creative Services department. "Just be sure you look like Cupid."

I took the problem home to my wife. Bonnie, when she stopped laughing, suggested that maybe she could make a costume. She started out with a rather large pair of red pantyhose. Then she recycled an old pale-gray sweatshirt of mine by glueing hot pink felt hearts of assorted sizes all over it. She did the same for an old pair of gray flannel gym shorts, then topped off the costume with a pair of wings—fashioned from wire coathangers and plastic wrap—sewn to the back of the sweatshirt.

I added a couple of my own touches: a pair of cowboy boots and my old battered red-and-white "One Tank Trips" hat. But what to do for a bow and arrow?

My friend Gary Rice of Lakewood is a teacher. He is also a packrat. A flea market maven, like me, if he doesn't have some object in his house, he knows where to get it.

"Gary," I said over the telephone, "I need a bow and arrow like Cupid carried."

Gary, who knows me well, didn't even ask why. "Let me think about it," he replied. "I'll call you back."

A half hour later, Gary came into my kitchen carrying a long package wrapped in an old duffel bag.

"I couldn't find exactly the type of bow and arrow that Cupid carried," Gary said as he unwrapped the package, "but I think this will do." He held up a large toilet plunger with feathers affixed to the handle, and a large steel object.

"I didn't have a bow," he apologized, "so I took the top part off a crossbow and put the string from an old bass fiddle on it."

My costume was complete.

The next day videographer Jim Holloway and I went to Sell's Candy Store in Bay Village to shoot the segments with me in my Cupid costume.

First, I discovered that trying to stand on one foot to assume the classic Cupid pose is hard work. (I also discovered that I looked like a fat flamingo.) I could stand on one foot for about thirty seconds before losing the pose. Jim would just get focused in and I would drop down to two feet, ruining his shot.

Then there were the customers, who would walk into the store and suddenly see me standing on one foot, wearing red pantyhose and carrying a steel bow with a toilet plunger for an arrow. Some snickered, some laughed out loud. One woman ran screaming from the store.

Finally, we finished with the taping, and several bystanders said they wanted to have their photo taken with me. We gathered close as Jim took the proffered camera and proceeded to point it at us. As we stood, arms around each other beaming at the camera, one of the women reached back and pinched me on the rear end and, as I jumped,with a shocked look on my face, the camera went off.

Later, on the air, Channel Eight anchor Robin Swoboda christened me "Doctor Love" amidst laughter on the set. I still get hailed by strangers who want to know where my bow and arrow are. I just blush and say I left them in my Nash Metropolitan.

As for those romantic getaways, here are the favorites:

Greenwood Inn.

SLEEP IN A 1959 CADILLAC CONVERTIBLE

Here are two dozen fantasy suites ranging from Cadillac Suite, where you actually sleep in a pink, 1959 Cadillac convertible, to the Far North, where the bedroom resembles the interior of an igloo with a round waterbed and bearskin rug for a cover. There is also Cinderella's Room, where you sleep in a full-sized carriage "pulled" by papier-machè horses. Another room has a full-sized Venetian gondola just wide enough for two.

Greenwood Inn and Fantasuite Hotel   ☎ 317-882-2211
1117 East Main Street • Greenwood, Ind. 46142
Location: Greenwood is a suburb just south of Indianapolis, IA
Handicapped access: Yes, to some rooms.

FROM VICTORIAN TO VEGAS

The seventy-plus fantasy suites here range from Victorian splendor to shipboard coziness. Some rooms appear to be in underground caves; others offer outdoor themes, such as the jungle or a small town, where you can sleep on the "front porch." The hotel also offers a fine dinner theater with a Vegas-style show that includes showgirls, dancing, and variety-show acts. The hotel is located across the street from Valley Forge National Park and is just minutes from downtown Philadelphia, so you can also enjoy some shopping and sightseeing.

The Sheraton-Valley Forge Hotel   ☎ 215-337-2000
First Avenue and North Gulph Road · King of Prussia, Pennsylvania 19406
Location: King of Prussia is a suburb of Philadelphia.
Handicapped access: Yes.

HOME OF THE CHAMPAGNE-GLASS WHIRLPOOL BATH

This resort is part of the famous Caesar's hotel chain and is an eastern Pennsylvania landmark. Rooms offer all the usual amenities, and some unusual ones, too: wood-burning fireplaces, two-story champagne glass whirlpool baths, two-person steam showers, a heart-shaped swimming pool (in your bedroom!), a massage table, and a round waterbed. Prices usually include all meals and entertainment.

Caesar's Brookdale on the Lake   ☎ 800-233-4141 or 717-226-2101
Pennsylvania Route 611 · Scotrun, Pennsylvania 18355
Location: In eastern Pennsylvania in the Pocono Mountains. Can be reached by the Pennsylvania Turnpike.
Handicapped access: Yes, to some rooms.

BED AND BREAKFAST IN A CASTLE

A brand-new castle built on a hill in Vinton County, not far from Hocking State Parks, Ravenwood offers rooms with king- or queen-sized beds, private bathrooms, and some with whirlpool baths. In the Great Room, breakfast is served, and later, for an additional cost, dinner in front of a roaring fireplace. This has become a very popular spot for weddings and honeymoons as well as regular romantic getaways.

Ravenwood Castle Bed and Breakfast   ☎ 800-477-1541
Ohio Route 1, Box 52-B • New Plymouth, Ohio 45654
Location: South of Hocking Hills and Old Man's Cave area, south of Lancaster, Ohio.
Handicapped access: Yes, to some rooms.

A SCOTTISH COUNTRY INN

This brand-new structure, built in the style of a sixteenth-century Scottish manor, is tucked away in the woods near the Hocking Hills Cave area. Besides the manor, the owner has also built several cabins in the woods, each located to insure privacy and equipped with fireplace, living room–kitchen, bedroom, and private bath. On a deck facing the woods is a giant wooden hot tub where you can sit at night and watch the stars. Rooms in the manor have fireplaces and whirlpool baths. Available at extra cost is a dinner for two; the host, dressed in a Scottish kilt, goes from table to table reading poetry to the ladies. No children allowed. The inn, they say, is "for lovers only." Special note: no smoking allowed in the buildings or on the grounds.

Glenlaurel, a Scottish Country Inn   ☎ 800-809-REST
15042 Mount Olive Road • Rockbridge, Ohio 43149
Location: Near Logan, Ohio, south of Columbus.
Handicapped access: Steps into cottages and some rooms.

SPEND THE NIGHT LIKE A POET

You can spend the night here in a replica of the homes of poets Edgar Allan Poe or Walt Whitman or, if there is a patriot in the family, Patrick Henry. This street of homes of famous Americans was built more than fifty years ago by auto maker Henry Ford, just as he was completing his Greenfield Village Museum. The idea was to make guest houses that duplicated the homes of famous Americans he admired. Today the homes are part of the Dearborn Inn and are available to the public by reservation. All have private baths, and some have been broken into two or three suites. Usual hotel amenities are provided.

Colonial Village: The Dearborn Inn   ☎ 313-271-2700
A Marriott Hotel
20301 Oakwood Boulevard • Dearborn, Michigan 48124
Location: In Dearborn, Michigan, just a few blocks from the Henry Ford Museum,
Greenfield Village complex.
Handicapped access: Steps in some houses.

Dearborn Inn. *Courtesy of Dearborn Inn.*

BED, BREAKFAST, AND GRAPES

If you like to visit wineries, here's one you don't have to leave! You can visit, take part in a wine tasting, and then spend the night in the winery, in a bedroom with private bath and your own private hot tub. This is a small family-owned winery; most of the wines are made from grapes grown on the property. The place is small and very informal. A continental breakfast is provided. Wine-tasting packages are offered.

Buccia Winery Bed and Breakfast   ☎ 216-593-5976
518 Gore Road • Conneaut, Ohio 44030
Location: Near Conneaut, Ohio, call for directions and reservations.
Handicapped access: Yes.

A DINNER TRAIN

This dinner train has a kitchen and chef on board. The specially built dining car has live entertainment, and white tablecloth and napkin service. The train goes only six or seven miles through a wooded swamp and then returns, but the night we were on board at least one couple became engaged and a few others looked very close. The music, the wine, the food, and the countryside sliding by outside combine for a nice romantic surprise for your significant other. And if you can't get enough of trains just riding on this one, for an extra fee you can sleep in a real railroad sleeping car parked in the station.

Star Clipper Dinner Train and Bed and Breakfast   ☎ 810-960-9440
840 North Pontiac Trail • Walled Lake, Michigan 48390
Location: Near Detroit, Michigan, not far from I-96.
Handicapped access: Steps into train and on train.

MORE ROMANCE

56 Great Places to Get Away from It All

One of the questions I get asked most often is "Where can I find a nice place to just get away with my husband/wife/boyfriend/girl-friend/significant other?" To answer that, I decided to sift through the last eighteen years of research and list some really nice places that I have visited but that for one reason or another didn't make it into my earlier book or fit elsewhere in this one. So here they are, in no particular order. Most are in rural areas. All offer private bathrooms, unless I note otherwise.

A LOVE BOAT WITH WINGS

"Your own little Love Boat with wings" is what Captain Dave McDonald calls the single-engine plane, capable of carrying up to six people, that is the sole aircraft of his Cincinati-based Flamingo Airlines.

McDonald is filling a niche in the airline industry: day trips on specialty flights. For example, he offers one quick down-in-the-morning, back-in-the-afternoon shopping flight to Gatlinburg, Tennessee, and an afternoon shopping flight to Cleveland. For those who enjoy something a little more colorful, he offers a quick flight to Chicago, where you are met at the airport by a limousine that whisks you on a whirlwind tour of the spots once frequented by gangster Al Capone and other infamous Chicago mobsters. But Dave's real claim to fame and most successful flight so far is called "Flights of Fancy."

Dave says this flight is for romantics. The plane carries only a pilot and two passengers—you and your significant other. The middle row of seats is removed and replaced by large satin pillows. There is a rose, a box of chocolates, a bottle of champagne, and a curtain that blocks the pilot's view of the back of the aircraft. There is also, according to Dave, a "very, very, discreet pilot." The plane takes off and climbs over a mile in the sky, circling over the Ohio

River for an hour before returning to its home base at Lunken Airport.

Just how popular is the flight? Dave says that after a local paper printed a story about his service last Valentine's Day, he was booked solid for three months.

McDonald says that while his pilots are the epitome of discretion, some things do draw their attention. Like the evening one pilot was flying a couple on a Flight of Fancy and the curtain suddenly fell or was accidentally kicked down, landing in the empty passenger seat next to the pilot. A long, naked leg stretched between the seats and retrieved the curtain, and moments later it was back in place.

There was also the time Dave was flying along at about 5,500 feet over the river, when he was kicked in the back of the head by a couple in the back of the plane who had become a bit rambunctious. Also, more than one champagne cork has bounced off the pilot's head during flight.

"They really do have a lot of privacy back there," Dave McDonald says. "Besides, I'm so busy flying the plane, I don't have time to think about what's happening." As for eavesdropping on his passengers, Dave points out that the roar of the motor covers most sounds, and he is also wearing a pair of earphones and listening to air traffic controllers in the Cincinnati area. "Like I said," McDonald continues, "it's their own little Love Boat, but with wings."

Call for rates and reservations. Pickups can be scheduled at Cleveland's Burke Lakefront Airport for an extra fee.

Flamingo Airlines   ☎ 513-871-8600, ext. 146
Lunken Airport
358 Wilmer Avenue • Cincinnati, Ohio 45226
Location: About five miles east of downtown Cincinnati, along the Ohio River.
Handicapped access: Steps into airplane.

A HISTORIC CINCINNATI BED AND BREAKFAST

This grand old home is located on a street of historic homes just across the Ohio River from downtown Cincinnati. It's especially appreciated by executives visiting Cincinnati who don't want to stay in a big hotel, with all the hassles of parking and tipping. The home has been beautifully restored, with high ceilings and chandeliers that look like something out of a movie. There is a bridal suite with gas fireplace and whirlpool tub, but all the regular rooms are nice, too, including several in an old barn, where you sleep in a former horse stall. There are no phones in the rooms, but there is television. They also serve a full breakfast, not a skimpy "continental" thing with juice and toast. Reservations are a must here almost any time of year.

Amos Shinkle Townhouse Bed and Breakfast
☎ 800-972-7012 or 606-431-2118
215 Garrard Street • Covington, Kentucky 41011
Location: In downtown Covington, across the river from Cincinnati, Ohio.
Handicapped access: Steps to upper floors.

A MODERNIZED VICTORIAN

This Victorian home has been modernized: all rooms now have private baths, some have whirlpools, gas fireplaces, and balconies. The big selling point here is the location—just across the street from Atwood Lake in southeast Ohio. It's also not far from New Philadelphia, and the outdoor drama *Trumpet in the Land*. The owners also offer gourmet breakfasts and dinners for an extra charge. The house is filled with antique glassware.

Whispering Pines Bed and Breakfast   ☎ 330-735-2824
State Route 542 • Dellroy, Ohio 44620
Location: Right next to Atwood Lake.
Handicapped access: Steps to some rooms.

STAY ON A QUIET COUNTRY ROAD

This B & B is located halfway between Berlin and Wooster, on a quiet country road with Amish neighbors all around. The owner is a pastor in a local church. He built this home for his family and then added a wing when they decided to go into the bed and breakfast business. Bedrooms have twelve-foot-high ceilings, large French doors that lead onto a balcony, gas fireplaces, giant whirlpool tubs, and a full private bath. All rooms appear to have been professionally decorated. The house sits in the middle of five acres of lawn, and the bedrooms overlook a large lake. Visitors are encouraged to go boating and fishing on the lake. All rooms have a private entrance. Children are allowed, but no pets. They do accept credit cards.

Gilead's Balm Manor Bed and Breakfast ☎ 330-695-3881
8690 County Road 201 • Fredericksburg, Ohio 44627
Location: In northern Holmes County; ask for a map when making reservations.
Handicapped access: Yes.

A LAKE ERIE VIEW

This B & B on the edge of Lake Erie was built about forty years ago as the home of a local doctor. The bedrooms are all air-conditioned and have private baths. There is a hot tub on a screened porch overlooking Lake Erie. A gazebo on the lawn is a great place to sit and read, or just watch boats go by.

Charlma Bed and Breakfast ☎ 216-466-3646
6739 Lake Road, West • Geneva-on-the-Lake, Ohio 44041
Location: On edge of Lake Erie, just west of Geneva-on-the-Lake.
Handicapped access: Steps to second-floor bedrooms.

A MENNONITE GUEST HOUSE

A Mennonite couple and their children run this huge log home, which they built as a guest house. All the rooms have whirlpool baths, are decorated in different themes, and offer the solitude of a country back road. Some of the rooms have gas fireplaces. The front porch faces a pasture and a bend in the road; you can sit out here for hours watching horse-drawn buggies go by while listening to some classical music piped throughout the common rooms of the home.

Fields of Home Guest House and Bed and Breakfast ☎ 330-674-7152
7278 County Road 201 • Millersburg, Ohio 44654
Location: On a side road north of Berlin, Ohio. Ask for map when making reservations.
Handicapped access: Yes, ramps and first-floor rooms.

A NEW BED AND BREAKFAST IN AMISH COUNTRY

This is one of the newest bed and breakfasts in Amish country. It is the former home of a local doctor. Each bedroom has a private bath, and one has a large whirlpool. What sets the Port Washington apart is the indoor swimming pool (in a separate building). The Amish manager serves what she calls a "continental breakfast, plus" that includes several fresh-squeezed juices and fresh-baked pastries, along with cereal and fresh fruit. There are two large fireplaces in the living room, and large decks off the back of the home overlooking miles of trees and farmland.

The Port Washington Inn
4667 Township Road 312 (also known as Port Washington Road)
Millersburg, Ohio 44654
Location: Just outside of Millersburg, Ohio.
Handicapped access: Yes.

RANCH BED AND BREAKFAST

This is a bit rustic, but if you are a horse lover it might be just right for you. It's an old farmhouse that has been given a Western touch. There is also a cabin with a wood-burning stove, kitchen, and private bath. The horses are the big selling point here. There are riding lessons in an enclosed arena, trail rides, and, weather permitting, horse-drawn sleigh rides in the winter. If you are a novice, there are lessons. If you are an experienced horse-person, spirited horses are available—but you have to prove to the head wrangler you know your way around a horse before they let you saddle up.

Spring Valley Ranch Bed and Breakfast   ☎ 814-489-5657
U.S. Route 6 • Spring Valley, Pennsylvania
Location: On U.S. Route 6 about 45 minutes southeast of Erie, Pennsylvania.
Handicapped access: Yes to cabin.

IF YOU LIKE THE FURNITURE, TAKE IT WITH YOU

This is another new operation in Amish country. The rooms are all furnished with locally handmade furniture, and it's all for sale; you can buy copies of any of the furniture you see at a shop at the rear of the inn. All the rooms are air conditioned and have private baths. Special here are the package deals. One offers a night in the bed and breakfast and a candlelight dinner for two at a real Amish home. During the winter, a package includes a horse-drawn sleigh ride with a night's stay. In the summer, you can get an Amish buggy ride along with your room. At breakfast some unusual bakery items are served, like "pumpkin whoopee pies."

Carriage Haus Inn   ☎ 330-893-2226
5453 East Street • Berlin, Ohio 44610
Location: In downtown Berlin, Ohio.
Handicapped access: Yes.

A HISTORIC HIDEAWAY

Looking for a weekend hideaway that combines history with comfort and good food? This is the place. The Spread Eagle Tavern has stood in this small community since before the Civil War. In recent years it has had a rebirth thanks to its current owners, who have poured hundreds of thousands of dollars into the building to keep it looking as it did when canal boats would glide by and passengers might stop to spend the night. Many prominent Republicans have stopped here, including former president George Bush, former vice president Dan Quayle, and presidential contender Bob Dole. Why do they choose this out-of-the-way spot for dinner or a night's sleep? The owner is the county Republican chairman. All of them have probably been pleased with the renovated inn, which now boasts private baths, gas fireplaces, four-poster beds, and an award-winning kitchen. One of the oddities of the place, besides the rumors of a friendly ghost, is in the cellar pub. On the wall is a death mask of 1930s gangster "Pretty Boy" Floyd. Floyd was shot and killed by the F.B.I. and local police not far from here. The local undertaker made the mask while preparing Floyd's body for shipment back to his family in Oklahoma.

One of the more pleasant places to eat lunch on a nice day is in the tiny courtyard just outside the kitchen. Nearby is the smokehouse where they smoke their own meats, like hams, pheasants, and turkeys. The aroma is wonderful.

Be sure to make reservations; this is a very popular spot and sometimes is booked months in advance.

Spread Eagle Tavern & Inn   ☎ 216-223-1583
10150 Plymouth Street • Hanoverton, Ohio 44423
Location: Off U.S. 30, east of Canton.
Handicapped access: Steep steps to second floor and to the basement pub.

STAY AT OHIO'S LEAST-KNOWN STATE PARK

This is one of Ohio's least-known state parks. And one of the loveliest. A small village has been re-created near a lock on the old Sandy Canal, which once ran through here. You can climb to the top of one of the locks and do what lockkeepers did a hundred years ago: close the huge wooden locks by hand to allow water to run into the chamber, raising canal boats several feet to get them to the next level of the river. There is also an old gristmill and a one-room schoolhouse that looks as though the children left just moments before. There are wonderful walking trails throughout the park, and this is one of the few facilities in the state that allows camping with your horse. On the edge of the park you can see the historical marker where 1930s-era gangster "Pretty Boy" Floyd was gunned down by lawmen. In another area of the park, you can find an abandoned village where, it is said, the ghost of a young woman still walks, searching for her betrothed who never returned from the Civil War.

Beaver Creek State Park   ☎ 216-385-3091
Route 1, Echo Dell Road · East Liverpool, Ohio 43920
Location: On Ohio Route 7, just north of East Liverpool, Ohio.
Handicapped access: Yes.

INDIAN TEEPEE RENTALS

How about a romantic night in an authentic Native American teepee? Well, somewhat authentic; this tent is already set up on a wooden deck (no sleeping on the ground here) and has electricity, but that's about it. You're not allowed to build a fire inside the tent like the Indians did; the fire ring is located outside for safety reasons. A bathroom with running water and shower is located in a nearby building. Bring along your own blankets, or deer hides, and food.

Mohican State Park   ☎ 419-994-5125
P.O. Box 22 · Loudonville, Ohio 44842
Location: Mohican State Park is located near Ashland and Mansfield in north central Ohio.
Handicapped access: Yes.

ANTIQUES

57 An Antique Store You Can Sleep In

If you like to use your antiques, not just look at them, I might have just the place for you. It's an antique store that lets you try out the antiques before you buy them. It's also a very beautiful bed and breakfast.

John Foos Manor. *Courtesy of John Foos Manor.*

The John Foos Manor is a landmark in Springfield, Ohio. Once owned by one of the leading families in the city, this Italianate mansion has been preserved to look much like it did when it was built in the 1870s. From its dramatic front hallway to the sixteen-foot-tall doors, the Manor is a tribute to the architectural styles of the late nineteenth century. But what makes this place stand out from other mansions-turned-bed-and-breakfasts is that here, if you like the furniture in your bedroom, you can buy it and take it home.

By day, the John Foos Manor operates as an antique gallery. But when guests are registered, public access ceases at 6:00 p.m., and only the guests are allowed in the building. All the antiques are for sale. Each piece is marked, and guests are encouraged to tour the house in the evening, including the bedrooms that are not occupied. A warehouse at the rear of the property has spare beds and other pieces of furniture to quickly replace any that might be sold to an overnight guest.

Several rooms have private baths, including one that has the most unusual shower stall I have ever seen—it looks like a plumber's fantasy, with faucets that will spray every part of the human body. There are also several pleasant areas on the patio and in the garden in which to sit and read.

John Foos Manor   ☎ 513-323-3444
810 East High Street • Springfield, Ohio 45505
Handicapped access: Steps into home, but there is an elevator to upper floors.

OHIO'S LARGEST ANTIQUE MALL (THEY CLAIM)

This place bills itself as "Ohio's Largest Antique Mall." I don't know about that, but it is very big. The relatively new building contains upwards of 400 individual dealers who have rented space to display their specialties. The owner is physically challenged and has made sure that the place is wheelchair accessible. There are nice wide aisles, good lighting, and handicapped-accessible bathrooms. There is also a lobby with a huge chandelier and fireplace where members of the family who are not into antiques can sit by the fire and relax or read. There is also a small snack area with vending machines.

As for the antiques, there is a good selection of everything from silver and glass to big items like architectural antiques and furniture. You can also bargain. Management has the right to wheel and deal to a certain extent, but if you insist, they will pass along any offers that they refuse to the dealers and let them make the final decision.

Springfield Antique Mall   ☎ 513-322-8868
1735 Titus Road (I-70 & U.S. 40) • Springfield, Ohio 45505
Location: Just outside of Springfield, Ohio, on I-70. (You can see it from the highway.)
Handicapped access: Yes.

OHIO'S *OTHER* LARGEST ANTIQUE MALL

This place *also* claims to be the biggest antique mall in Ohio, and in sheer size it may be. Located in an abandoned discount store, it spills over seventy thousand square feet! It's so big the aisles have street names, just like a small city. More than 300 dealers have their merchandise on display, everything from a complete 1920s barbershop to petroleum collections to the usual furniture and glass and silver collectibles. Delivery can be arranged for large items. A back room houses scratch-and-dent antiques that are on sale. There are restrooms and a snack bar. Open seven days a week.

Riverfront Antique Mall   ☎ 800-247-3704
I-77 and Ohio Route 39 • New Philadelphia, Ohio 44463
Location: At the edge of the Tuscarawas River on the west side of New Philadelphia by I-77.
Handicapped access: Yes.

YET *ANOTHER* LARGEST ANTIQUE MALL

This is owned by the same people who operate the Springfield Antique Mall. With 300-plus dealers all under one roof, it was once known as the "Largest Antique Mall in Northwest Ohio". It sells all types of antiques; many of the dealers specialize in one thing, like silver or glassware. Restrooms. Open seven days a week.

Jeffrey's Antique Gallery   ☎ 419-423-7500
11326 Township Road 99 • Findlay, Ohio 45840
Location: Near Findlay exit on I-75.
Handicapped access: Yes.

POTTERY AND ANTIQUES

More than 200 dealers are gathered in an abandoned department store in downtown East Liverpool. A specialty is local pottery. East Liverpool was once the pottery-making capital of Ohio. Several of the local potteries also have outlet stores inside this mall and offer discontinued series or seconds at discounted prices.

Pottery City Galleries, Antique and Collectible Mall
☎ 330-385-6933 or 800-380-6933
409 Washington Street • East Liverpool, Ohio 43920
Location: Near the center of East Liverpool, Ohio, on the Ohio River.
Handicapped access: Yes.

ANTIQUE CAPITAL OF MICHIGAN

This tiny Southeast Michigan town is mostly antique stores. Some of the most interesting ones are found in the old town hall, where, in addition to displays of antiques for sale, there is a museum dedicated to old toys, Native Americans, and other assorted subjects. On the street is one of my favorite stores—an old bookstore, where there was once a box to put the money in if you bought something. It was all on the honor system. The owner just opened the door in the morning and let people browse through the old books; if you found something you liked, the price was marked on the book and you just put the money in the box and took the book home.

Old Allen Township Hall Shops   ☎ 517-869-4891 or 517-278-6485
114 West Chicago Road • Allen, Michigan 49227
Location: Southeast lower Michigan, not far from the Ohio border.
Handicapped access: Yes, to some stores.

FLEA MARKETS

58 Fleas, and Other Bargains

It was about ten years ago that I first discovered flea markets. I have been a hardcore flea-market junkie ever since. My garage literally overflows with some of my better flea-market purchases. Like the lava lamp that no longer churns—a bargain at two dollars. Or the portable CD player that the previous owner assured me had only been used a week. (He forgot to mention that it had been used by a four-year-old who thought it was a hockey puck.) My shelves bulge with other bargains, like twenty new windsocks, all in purple and green, that were a bargain because they were sewn shut! Or the movie video I bought from a man who told me he had only viewed the film once. It turned out to be a very poor quality home copy, with most of the dialogue missing.

My wife, Bonnie, looks upon flea-market merchandise as "junk, just junk." She long ago gave up accompanying me on my weekly mission to do my bit for Mother Earth by reclaiming some person's cast-off and giving it a new chance at a useful life. This is fine with Bonnie, as long as I agree not to bring any of my "finds" into the house.

Over the years I have managed to disregard this edict and, each week, I return from a trip to the flea market with my latest trophy grasped tightly in my hot, sweaty hands. A few weeks later I know I will find my treasure sitting in the garage, put there by my loving wife, a mute suggestion that the "treasure" be returned to the flea market to find a new owner.

Occasionally, when the pile of merchandise threatens to displace our cars from the garage, I load up the station wagon with boxes of these wondrous things and venture out to the weekend flea markets to become a seller instead of a buyer. I have been told by people experienced in selling that the secret to making money at the flea market is to buy low and sell high. Somehow I usually wind up selling for lower than I bought. I am so uncertain about my sales ability that usually when someone stops at my booth and offers half of what I have marked on the item, I, like a bad poker player, quickly accept the price and make no attempt at a counter-proposal. And there are those broken items I have purchased. Even though I mark them "as is" I feel compelled to confess to a prospective buyer that this item probably belongs in the trash can and not on my counter. The end result is usually a lost sale.

Still, I am hooked by the stories of others who revel in real flea-market finds: the valuable painting found behind a piece of cardboard in a ten-dollar frame; the old suitcase, purchased for a dollar, containing piles of valuable bonds, worth thousands of dollars; an old vase that turns out to be one in a thousand, its value inestimable. These stories flow up and down the aisles at a flea market. Sadly, it is always someone else who makes these finds, but the fact that they exist propels me out of bed before dawn on flea-market day. The stories have taken me through cold rainy dawns, plodding through puddles, cold and miserable, hoping to make the big find. All, I might add, without success. But the early bird gets the worm, and I find much company in the predawn hours at a flea market. There is a camaraderie as the regulars exchange notes about the finds that got away because they got to a seller just moments too late.

I am still haunted by the morning that I spied an older, but still quite valuable camera, lying in a box beside the open trunk of a car. The seller seemed mostly interested in keeping warm and chewing up a large donut as I sidled up and asked him, "How much for the camera?" He held up five fingers, and knowing the value of the camera, I assumed he was saying five hundred dollars, which would have been a fair price. While I was debating whether to make the purchase, another man stepped up from behind me and asked the seller, "Do you mean five dollars?" The seller nodded. Before I could even open my mouth to object, the man bent down, scooped up the camera, shoved a five-dollar bill in the seller's hand, and literally ran off with it before the seller could change his mind. I was left standing with my mouth open, sputtering like a motorboat.

If you are going to a flea market, keep the following tips in mind:

1. Don't be afraid to offer less than the asking price for something you see. The seller won't be offended. That's what flea markets are all about—bargaining.

2. If the item is electrical or mechanical, be sure to try it before you buy it. Remember, you are not buying a new item. (Why do you think that object ended up at the flea market in the first place?) If you don't check it out, and it doesn't work, don't complain. Let the buyer beware.

3. Understand what you are buying. Most things at a flea market are sold "as is," and that means exactly what it says. Most vendors do not have a return or exchange policy. Once the money changes hands, it's yours, forever.

4. Wear comfortable shoes when shopping, especially in the larger flea markets, where you might end up walking five miles or more among the vendors.

5. Bring along a net bag or something else to carry your purchases in. Many vendors do not have bags or boxes to give you.

6. Bring cash. Most vendors will not accept checks and very few ever take credit cards.

7. If you find that object you have been looking for all your life and you don't have the money on you to purchase it, you might try asking the vendor to take it off the counter and hold it until you can get to a bank. You may be asked to make a deposit to hold it, though.

8. If someone beats you to the buy of the day, relax—there is always another flea market and more bargains to be had next week.

While we don't have the year-round open-air flea markets of the sunshine belt, we do have several that operate indoors in inclement weather and expand three- and fourfold when the weather is warm. Here are some of the best in Ohio and nearby states.

SHIPSHEWANA FLEA MARKET

Open every Tuesday and Wednesday, with an auction on Wednesday, this is one of the Midwest's larger flea markets. On a nice summer day, upwards of a thousand vendors will be set up in fields surrounding the auction barn. The outside market is closed down from November until early spring.

Shipshewana Flea Market ☎ 219-768-4129
345 South Van Buren Street • Shipshewana, Indiana
Location: Northeast Indiana, near Indiana Turnpike.
Handicapped access: Gravel walkways.

JAMIE'S FLEA MARKET

Open Wednesday and Saturday year round. It has permanent buildings, and during warm weather several hundred additional vendors set up on one side of the parking lot and around the front of the market property. There is usually a good mix, from folks selling from the trunks of their automobiles to established vendors who specialize in tools, antiques, or other specialty items. The parking lot is unpaved, and on busy days after a rain it can get a bit muddy. Bring boots. This flea market has been a Lorain County landmark for more than twenty-five years.

Jamie's Flea Market ☎ 216-986-4402
Ohio Route 113 • South Amherst, Ohio 44001
Location: Northeast Ohio, west of Cleveland, near I-90 and Ohio Turnpike.
Handicapped access: Some paved areas near vendors.

THE HARTVILLE FLEA MARKET

Open every Monday and Thursday year round. Permanent buildings with longtime vendors that sell fresh meats, produce, and many other items. In the warm seasons, the parking lots are filled with hundreds of vendors selling from trucks, cars, and tents. Just across the road is the beautiful new multi-million-dollar restaurant, the Hartville Kitchen, a favorite with visitors to the flea market.

The Hartville Flea Market ☎ 216-877-9353
788 Edison Street • Hartville, Ohio 44632
Location: North central Ohio between Akron and Canton, near I-77.
Handicapped access: Some gravel walkways and inclines. Steps into some buildings.

CAESAR'S CREEK FLEA MARKET

Open every Saturday and Sunday year round. Permanent buildings for regular vendors. Everything from furniture to fresh produce. During good weather, hundreds of other vendors set up around the buildings and throughout the parking lot.

Caesar's Creek Flea Market   ☎ 513-382-1669
I-71 and Ohio Route 73 • Wilmington, Ohio
Location: Southwest Ohio, between Columbus and Cincinnati, close to I-71.
Handicapped access: Gravel parking lots, some paved areas.

ROGERS FLEA MARKET

This flea market and auction operates every Friday year round. Several buildings house vendors and an auction, and in warmer weather upwards of a thousand vendors set up outside, surrounding the buildings. This event attracts residents from three states. Parking lots are often some distance from flea market. Get there early in the day for close-in parking during peak season.

Rogers Flea Market   ☎ 216-227-3233
Ohio Route 7 • Rogers, Ohio
Location: Just off Ohio Route 7, north of East Liverpool, Ohio.
Handicapped access: Some paved walkways, but also many gravel and dirt areas, especially on busy days.

MEMPHIS DRIVE-IN THEATER AND FLEA MARKET

This is one of my favorites. On a nice Saturday or Sunday morning upwards of four hundred dealers pack this outdoor theater. It's a good mix of true dealers and just plain folks who are cleaning out the garage and attic. I have had some of my best finds here. It's also open on Wednesdays, but the crowd is usually much smaller. There is an admission charge for buyers and sellers. There are inside bathrooms, a refreshment stand, and lots of electrical outlets for trying out those gadgets before you buy them.

Memphis Drive-In Theater and Flea Market   ☎ 216-941-2892
10543 Memphis Avenue • Brooklyn, Ohio 44144
Location: Suburb on west side of Cleveland.
Handicapped access: Gravel and paved roadway.

PRISONS

59 Spend Your Vacation Behind Bars

The first time I was in the Mansfield Reformatory, I was there to do a story on the inmates' formation of a behind-the-walls Rotary Club chapter. I had even received a written invitation to be their speaker. I accepted partly out of curiosity and, also, because it seemed like a good feature story. On the day of the visit, after the meeting, one of the guard captains gave me a quick tour of the prison. It is a gothic-style building that is instantly depressing, even from the outside.

Being on the inside was even worse. The captain took me to one of the cell blocks, which was six stories high. The prisoners were mostly at work, and the tiny cells were all standing open. We had climbed the winding steel stairs to the sixth range and walked down the steel grid walkway, where I could look down all the way to the cement floor at ground level.

I asked if I could step into one of the cells and see what it must be like to be inside. The captain motioned to me to help myself. I walked inside one about halfway down the long corridor. It seemed to grow even smaller as I entered; I could almost touch the walls on both sides. The only furnishings were a one-piece steel toilet, a wash basin, and two folding cots attached to the wall. Gray blankets covered both beds, and there were small piles of personal possessions—magazines, candy bars, paperback books—stacked on the floor near the bunks. The smell was what really hit me—a cross between stale food and body odor. Paint on the steel walls was flaking off because of the humidity.

As I was turning around to leave, the door suddenly slid shut with a slam! The captain had activated the electronic locking device to show me what it was really like to be locked in a cell. My heart was pounding, my chest was tight, and I could feel claustrophobia building; I almost wanted to scream out as I grabbed the bars and looked through. I must confess that I was very happy to hear the captain say "Stand clear!" and see the door slide open again. I quickly left the cell and the range, and really had no desire to ever visit a prison again, until the summer of 1996.

By then, the Mansfield Reformatory had finally been closed and had been taken over by a historic preservation group that was raising money by giving guided tours of the old prison. I decided to visit once more.

The twenty-five-foot stone wall that surrounded the prison is gone, leaving the gothic buildings, battered by several years of neglect, exposed. Windows are broken, and the interior seems even more ragged because of the peeling water-based paints used by the movie company that used the prison as the set for the movie *The Shawshank Redemption.*

A retired prison guard, now working as a tour guide, took videographer Jim Holloway and me into the prison. As we approached the cell blocks, they seemed even more threatening and desolate than they did all those years ago. Missing were the sounds of life. Now all that could be heard was the chirp of birds that had flown in through broken windows. It was a fascinating tour as the guard told tales of criminals, famous and infamous, who once were imprisoned here—including one prisoner, a baseball player on the prison team, who was so good that scouts from the Detroit Tigers showed up at the prison to watch him play; when he was released, they gave him a job. But when we climbed to the sixth range of the cell block, I again felt the claustrophobic feeling I had had years ago and opted to skip that part of the tour, instead going for a look at the solitary cells in the basement and wandering through the prison gift shop, where souvenirs are now sold to tourists.

The preservation society hopes that the tours will produce enough money to help restore the old prison and preserve it as a reminder of what criminal justice in this country once was. Recently, the tour schedule was for Sundays only, but give them a call, schedules do change and groups can probably arrange for tours on other days.

At last report, there was still no heat in the building, so on cool days wear a sweater. Because of the thickness of the stone walls, it will seem much cooler inside. There is an admission charge.

The Mansfield Reformatory ☎ 419-522-2644
Mansfield Reformatory Preservation Society
100 Reformatory Road · P.O. Box 8625 · Mansfield, Ohio 44906-8625
Location: On the north side of U.S. 30 in Mansfield.
Handicapped access: No, lots of stairs to climb.

THE TOUGHEST PRISON IN WEST VIRGINIA

Termed the "toughest prison in West Virginia," this place held the "baddest of the bad" for 130 years. The four-story prison has two main sections, North Hall and South Hall, with a total of eight hundred cells. North Hall, where the incorrigibles were housed, used only every other cell, leaving cells in between empty to keep the inmates from passing contraband back and forth. During its long history, the prison saw several riots and even a few jailbreaks, the last one coming in the 1990s shortly before it was finally closed to make way for a new modern prison facility some miles away. In that last breakout, several prisoners working in a greenhouse inside the prison started offering free potted plants to guards. It was later discovered that they were tunneling under the greenhouse and under the prison wall to freedom, and were using the potted plants to get rid of dirt from their tunnel! When the jailbreak occurred they made one mistake: bad timing. They made it under the wall and then dug straight up, breaking through right beside the highway, where a school bus was just stopping to let off children. The driver alerted prison guards, and all the prisoners were recaptured.

West Virginia Penitentiary.

Nearly a hundred people were executed in this prison. The old gatehouse is the original 1863 prison, a four-story-high structure where the hangings were held. The gallows are still in place today. In fact, as part of the tour, now that the prison is a tourist attraction, guides trip the gallows and surprise visitors as a dummy falls through the hole in the floor and starts swinging on the end of the rope.

In the middle part of this century, the state switched to using the electric chair, until executions were outlawed in West Virginia. The little-used electric chair sits in the prison gift shop today, surrounded by a railing to keep people from posing for pictures in it.

Tours are conducted by former guards and residents from Tuesday through Sunday. The prison is closed during some winter months. Call for current hours. There is an admission charge. Cameras are allowed.

West Virginia State Penitentiary   ☎ 304-845-6200
818 Jefferson Avenue (corner of 8th and Jefferson) • Moundsville, West Virginia
Location: Downtown Moundsville is just 20 minutes from Wheeling, West Virginia.
Handicapped access: To some areas. All tours are on the first floor, but there are steps into some buildings.

A JAILHOUSE BED AND BREAKFAST

This actually was the county jail until the early 1900s. In fact, the courtyard (where breakfast is served in nice weather) was once the site of the gallows, where several people were executed. The oldest part of the jail, dating from the early 1800s, was made of wood and concrete; the walls are nearly three feet thick. Several beautifully decorated bedrooms have been made out of this part of the jail, and the thickness of the walls guarantees privacy. The newer section of the jail, in the back of the building, was used in later years to hold women prisoners, and the cells are roomy, with private baths. They have been redecorated, and have proven to be very popular with guests who want to say they spent the night in a jail cell. The cell doors are still there, but the keys are now left in the locks.

Jailer's Inn   ☎ 502-348-5551 or 502-348-3703
111 West Stephen Foster Avenue • Bardstown, Kentucky 40004
Location: In downtown Bardstown, Kentucky.
Handicapped access: Some steps.

SECTION II
State by State ...

OHIO

60 One of Amish Country's Dark Secrets

Driving through the tiny town of Ragersville, not far from Sugarcreek, in Ohio's Amish land, you would think this land of picturesque farms, white town halls, neat homes, and manicured lawns has always been this peaceful. But this town has a skeleton in the closet, literally. This quiet town once was the site of a lynching.

Jeff Davis was not a nice man. He had fourteen convictions for various crimes in his life. He was crude and coarse in his dealings with people, especially women. But what may have caused him to be the victim of a lynch mob may have been nothing more than a very bad attitude.

I first learned of Jeff Davis about fifteen years ago when some human bones were found in a building belonging to a recently deceased farmer in Berlin. They were taken to the Cuyahoga County coroner's office, which, after investigation, said they were those of a man who had been dead for over a century. How, I asked Holmes County Sheriff's Captain Arlie Croskey, did these bones end up in the farmer's building? And whose bones were they?

Croskey said it was suspected they were the bones of Jeff Davis, who had been hung by a mob in 1873 in the town of Ragersville.

Although the incident had happened 107 years earlier, I set off for Ragersville determined to find out just who Jeff Davis was and why they had done such a terrible thing to him.

What I found there was that many folks claimed to have never heard of him, some admitted they knew about the lynching but were reluctant to discuss it, and a few admitted that their ancestors may have taken part in it. From a variety of sources, I scraped this story together.

Jeff Davis turned up in the Ragersville area a half dozen years after the end of the Civil War. His name may have been an alias. He had also served time in the Ohio penitentiary as John Foanbieger, John Smith, and Richard Roe. It's thought his real name was Miller. In any event, the short, stocky Jeff Davis had a bad habit of using foul language and, when in the area of a town, grabbing at women he passed. In one instance, he was fined and sentenced to fifteen days on a chain gang for approaching a Miss Taylor and "making indecent grabs with his hands on her body and wanting her to kiss him."

As for the two village policemen who arrested him, he told them that when he got out of jail he would look them up and "cut their hearts out and feed them to the pigs."

So it is probably understandable that when Jeff Davis turned up in the town of Ragersville in August of 1873, townspeople were not happy about it. Just what happened next is a little hazy. Some reports say a young girl was raped, others say it was attempted rape, while still others say he simply grabbed a young girl as she walked by him. Whatever it was, it was too much for the townsfolk in Ragersville. That Saturday evening they gathered at the little wooden town hall at the end of the main street, next to the cemetery, to decide what to do about Jeff Davis.

It was a small town and Davis quickly learned about the meeting. He decided to attend it himself to see what was going on. That decision was the biggest mistake of his life.

Some reports say shots were fired as Davis walked in the door. Others say someone hit him over the head with a coal shovel. In any event, everyone agreed that somehow the coal oil lamps were extinguished, and when the lights came back on, Davis was on the floor, unconscious with a rope around him.

Mob rule took over. Davis was hauled out of the building and bounced down the steps into the dusty street, where the crowd fired several shots into his body. This woke him up and he began to plead for his life, as he was dragged through the streets of the village and finally to a tree near a brook at the edge of town. There, a rope was put around his neck and, still pleading and begging for mercy, Jeff Davis was hauled, kicking, to the highest limb, where he was hanged until dead.

A breeze in the night slowly twirled Davis's now still body. Villagers who moments before had been in a killing frenzy were regaining their senses and starting to realize what they had just done.

A horse and wagon were fetched. The body of Jeff Davis was cut down and tossed into the back of the wagon by two men who drove off into the night with it. Near Shanesville in Holmes County, just across the Tuscarawas County line, they stripped the corpse and buried it in a shallow grave on a small hill.

Several days later, Holmes County officials, hearing of the lynching, went looking for Davis's body. What they found was an empty grave.

It was later learned that a local doctor had also heard of the killing and the hillside burial; he had gone out, dug up Davis's body, taken it back to his home, and hidden it in his attic. This was an era when doctors had to steal bodies to do any medical research; the doctor apparently thought he might as well take advantage of the situation.

However, two days later, two cleaning women who were working at the doctor's house while he was away decided to surprise him by cleaning out his attic. As they raised the trapdoor to enter the attic, they found themselves face to face with the corpse of Jeff Davis (which by this time was getting a bit ripe). They ran screaming into the street just as the doctor arrived home. He decided it might be a good idea to get rid of the body, so he carried Jeff downstairs. Strapping him in a saddle on a swift horse, the doctor mounted a second, and went galloping out of town. The next morning, Davis's body was found lying on the front steps of the Ragersville town hall.

Another doctor then stepped in and said he would take care of the remains. He allegedly took it home, got out his huge copper cheese-making vat, and dragged it to a fire-pit in his backyard. He filled it with water, put Davis's body in the vat, and cooked it until all that was left was the skeleton. He then hung the skeleton in his office, where it remained for many years. It's believed the Berlin farmer ended up with the bones when he bought the contents of the doctor's office at auction following the doctor's death in the early years of this century.

Today there are still people who claim to have the original Jeff Davis skeleton, and there are other stories about how he died. One thing is certain, though: Ragersville, Ohio, in 1873 was not a good place to have a bad attitude.

Nowadays, of course, visitors to the Amish area are welcomed with open arms. It has become one of Ohio's fastest-growing tourist areas. Here are some great places to visit:

THE ONLY WINERY IN OHIO'S AMISH COUNTRY

At this, the only winery in Ohio's Amish country, Duke Bixler and his family specialize in berry, fruit, dandelion, and sparkling wines. The wines are still made in large barrels, and the sparkling wine is turned by hand. They have won many awards and are considered some of the best in Ohio. In an old barn on the property, the winery operates a gift shop that offers wine-tasting sessions, locally produced cheese, and Amish crafts. The family also operates a bed and breakfast in a century home. (However, we have not visited that property yet.)

Breitenbach Wine Cellars   ☎ 800-THE-WINE
Ohio Route 39 · Sugarcreek, Ohio 44681
Location: Just off Ohio Route 39, east of the town of Sugarcreek. Watch for the signs.
Handicapped access: Yes.

INLAND LIGHTHOUSES

This may seem like a strange attraction in Amish country, but more and more Amish craftsmen are making miniature lighthouses to sell to tourists. While the owner here is not Amish, he was one of the first to sell the lighthouses, and his products are available in a greater variety of sizes than those of some of the Amish. He also makes and sells gazebos for the lawn and cupolas for weathervanes. He always has several samples in front of his place of business for those people who don't want to wait for a custom-built one.

Midway Lighthouses   ☎ 330-263-0774
7505 Lincoln Way, East · Apple Creek, Ohio 44606
Location: On U.S. Route 30 between Wooster and Massillon
Handicapped access: Yes.

GUEST CABINS

These getaway cabins are operated by a Mennonite couple. Several recently built cabins are located around a small lake behind their home. While not luxurious, the cabins are clean and have electricity and bathrooms, a gas-fired fireplace, two bedrooms, a small dining and living room, and a porch to sit on and watch the sunsets from. Two things set this place apart. They welcome children (there is even a small playground near the edge of the lake), and they will accept pets, at an additional cost, if the pets are well behaved. This is a nice family getaway spot, nestled on a quiet side road surrounded by Amish and Mennonite farms.

Mel and Mary Raber's Cabins   ☎ 330-893-2695
2972 Township Road 190 • Baltic, Ohio 43804
Location: West of New Philadelphia, Ohio; call for directions.
Handicapped access: Yes.

FLOUR POWER

This mill has operated for more than one hundred years. Owner Alvin Miller still grinds his flour daily from grain that he has dried in large tubs out behind the mill. My wife, Bonnie, insists this is the only flour she has ever found that makes the perfect loaf of bread in a bread-making machine. Alvin also offers tours of the historic old mill. Closed on Sundays.

Baltic Mills   ☎ 330-897-0522
111 Main Street • Baltic, Ohio 43804
Location: In downtown Baltic, next to railroad tracks. Baltic is west of New Philadelphia, Ohio.
Handicapped access: Yes.

OHIO

61 The Superman of Amish Country

At first sight, Vernon Craig of Wilmot, Ohio, is not very imposing. He's a short, stout, pleasant man, balding, with a short beard that makes him appear to be either Amish or Mennonite. In other words, he blends right in with the majority of the population in these parts. His day job is managing a cheese and gift shop in the heart of the Amish lands of Ohio. Sounds like a pretty average person. But let me assure you, Vernon Craig is anything but average. Vernon, you see, has a secret identity, an alter ego. Vernon is also "The Amazing Komar."

Komar is the man who, decked out in a turban, silk pantaloons, and vest, set the world's record for the hottest fire walk in history. He walked, in his bare feet, across twenty-five feet of hot coals measured by a physicist at 1,494 degrees Fahrenheit! If you don't believe me, check the *Guinness Book of World Records*. And if that is not enough to impress, he also holds a world's record for lying between two beds of nails while supporting 1,642 pounds of weight! It's in the book, too. (By the way, the *Guinness* people have retired both records to discourage other people from trying to top Komar's records, because both feats are much too dangerous.)

You may have seen Komar on national television. He has appeared on many shows since the early 1970s, including a recent Fox Network show called "Wow! The Most Awesome Acts on Earth!" He was inducted into the World Record Hall Of Fame along with members of the Beatles, and statues of Komar are in most *Guinness Book of World Records* museums around the world. His fire-walking has taken him to more than 100 countries and six continents.

It all started back in 1963 when Vernon Craig, as Komar, was trying to use his skills to awaken interest in the mental health and mental retardation programs that he was then working in. Because of the attention he drew to the programs by his unusual skills, he was invited to Washington, D.C., by Senator Ted Kennedy to serve on the committee that organized and set up the Special Olympics Program.

Now grandfather Craig has retired from fire-walking and only occasionally demonstrates his ability to lie on a bed of nails and allow three or four people to stand on his chest and jump up and down. Many of Vernon Craig's neighbors in the Wilmot area, who are Amish, have no idea of his other identity as "The Amazing Komar." They simply know him as Vernon, the mild-mannered manager of the Alpine-Alpa Cheese Store. Just like Clark Kent.

ALPINE-ALPA: SWITZERLAND OVER HERE

This was one of the very first tourist attractions in Ohio's Amish Country. Started over sixty years ago by Alice Grossniklaus and her late husband, Hans, it is still one of the major attractions in the area. The complex today includes the original cheese-making plant, a restaurant, a cheese and gourmet shop, a bakery, and one of the largest cuckoo clock shops in the United States. The building also houses the world's largest cuckoo clock, 23 feet tall, 24 feet wide, and 13 feet deep. The cuckoo bird is 13 inches long. There are five animated figures who make up a Swiss band and dancers that are 36 to 42 inches high. The clock is in the *Guinness Book of World Records* and has been featured in *Ripley's Believe It or Not*.

As for the cheese (Swiss of course), Alpine-Alpa recently won an international contest that named their cheese the fourth best in the entire world!

A Swiss artist, the late Tom Miller, painted what he believed to be his masterpiece at Alpine-Alpa, turning the two-story-high dining room into a three-dimensional mural about Switzerland.

They are open seven days a week. If you stop in, be sure to say hello to Vernon Craig, a.k.a. "The Amazing Komar."

Alpine-Alpa: Switzerland Over Here   ☎ 330-359-5454
U.S. Route 62 • Wilmot, Ohio 44689
Location: Just south of the town of Wilmot on U.S. Route 62.
Handicapped access: Yes.

A POTATO CHIP FACTORY

This well-known local potato chip company has some real bargains in its company store. They usually have clear plastic bags filled with three pounds of chips that didn't make it through the inspection line. These sell at three for six dollars, which means you get nine pounds of chips for just six bucks! That's a bargain. The best part is that the chips are very fresh. They are considered "seconds" only because their color might be a bit dark (due to the sugar in the chip, not because it is burned) or because the chips are broken when they leave the production line. Other products are made here (such as caramel corn) that are not sold to distributors—they are only available locally. There are also pretzel "seconds"; nothing wrong with them, just broken. You can get a huge bag of pretzels for a couple of dollars. No tours of the potato chip plant are offered, but while in the outlet store just look to the rear and you'll see fresh, hot chips coming off the conveyor belt into containers.

Shearer Potato Chips ☎ 330-767-3426
692 Wabash Avenue (Ohio Route 93, North) • Brewster, Ohio 44613
Location: Brewster is south of Canton.
Handicapped access: Steps into store.

HANDMADE QUILTS

To see how some of the beautiful Amish-Mennonite quilts are made, watch the ladies sewing each day at this quilt shop. They will always answer questions and demonstrate how the intricately patterned quilts are made. There are hundreds of the quilts on display and for sale.

Gramma Fannie's Quilt Barn ☎ 330-893-3232
Box 270, Ohio Route 39 • Berlin, Ohio 44610
Location: On Ohio Route 39, east of the town of Berlin. It is a part of the Shrock's Amish Farm Complex.
Handicapped access: Steps into store and up to second floor.

'TIS ALWAYS THE SEASON HERE

This landmark building was constructed many years ago to house a cyclorama painting featuring Amish-Mennonite history. When the painting was finally finished, it was instead located in the Mennonite Information Center down the road. Since then the building has been used for a basketball court and an indoor arcade and now has begun a new life as a year-round Christmas store. The main rotunda is filled with beautifully decorated Christmas trees. A small chapel in the center of the building contains all types of angels and other decorations. Upstairs, overlooking the rotunda, a series of shops sells unusual gift items. For instance, one shop only sells gifts for professionals, including doctors, lawyers, teachers, as well as butchers, bakers, and candlestick makers.

'Tis the Season Year Round Christmas Shoppe ☎ 330-893-3232
Ohio Route 39 • Berlin, Ohio 44610
Location: On Ohio Route 39, east of Berlin, inside the Shrock's Amish Farm Complex.
Handicapped access: Yes.

BAG APPLE PIE

Although I mentioned this restaurant in my first book, I neglected to mention the dessert that has made it famous: Bag Apple Pie. This pie starts out with a normal pie shell, to which are added a dozen large Golden Delicious apples and a top of heavy cookie-dough crust. It is then baked in a paper bag to keep the cookie-dough top from burning. I don't know how it works, but what comes out is a pie that must weigh five pounds; a slice can be almost six inches high. Absolutely delicious!

The Dutch Harvest Restaurant ☎ 330-893-3000
Ohio Route 39, West • Berlin, Ohio 44610
Location: Just west of the town of Berlin, on Ohio Route 39.
Handicapped access: yes.

CRAFTSMANSHIP IN OAK AND CHERRY

If you want to see some Amish craftsmen at work making the beautiful oak and cherry furniture for which they are famous, you can do so in the salesroom at Dutch Heritage Woodcrafts. Through a large glass window you can look into the shop, where furniture is turned out one piece at a time. Inside you can choose from a fine selection of their products ready for sale, or you can custom order your furniture.

Dutch Heritage Woodcrafts ☎ 330-893-2211
Box 346, State Route 39 • Berlin, Ohio 44610
Location: On State Route 39 just east of the town of Berlin. It is part of the Shrock's Amish Farm Complex.
Handicapped access: Steps into store.

OHIO

62 Breakfast with the Governor

One of the questions I am often asked is "Why doesn't your wife travel with you?"

It's a fair question, and the answer is: she does travel with me, sometimes. My wife, Bonnie, has her own career as a registered nurse, and often our schedules do not mesh, so it usually is impossible for her to take advantage of the trips I make.

However, over the years we have been honored to be invited by Governor George Voinovich and his wife, Janet, to accompany them on what they refer to as familiarization tours. These are usually gatherings of a dozen or more travel journalists from across the nation whom the Voinoviches take time out of their busy schedule to lead around Ohio, showing them the tourist attractions of the Buckeye State and encouraging them to write about Ohio. During several of these trips, Governor and Mrs. Voinovich had mentioned that when Bonnie and I were in Columbus we should stop by and see the historic mansion that is the official residence of the state's chief executive.

Now, we had always believed that the Voinoviches were just being gracious and that the invitation wasn't really serious. I mean, think about it. Neil and Bonnie Zurcher just drop in at the Governor's Residence because we're in the neighborhood. Yeah, right.

Well, we had an attitude adjustment in December of 1996, when I had an appointment to do a story on the governor's newly renovated office in the statehouse. I was called one day, shortly before Christmas, and asked if I could do the story that Friday. I started to explain to the caller from the governor's office that I was on vacation when she said that if I could do the story then, the governor would personally lead the tour. I decided that I could spare a day of vacation to travel to Columbus. The next day I got another call from the governor's office. Since I was coming to Columbus, could my wife join me, and could both of us join the governor and Mrs.

Voinovich for breakfast at their residence before he went to the statehouse? I said yes. I guess they really meant those invitations.

When I got home that night I casually mentioned to Bonnie that the Friday before Christmas we were invited to have breakfast with the governor and his wife.

"What am I supposed to wear?" she asked.

"I don't know," I replied. "Clothes, I guess."

"You didn't even ask what we're supposed to wear?" she demanded.

Now, I must confess that I don't think much about clothes. People who know me well know that I consider "dressed up" to be a pressed set of faded denims and maybe a sweater over a faded favorite shirt. Actually, that's usually what I wear when I'm not dressed up, too. My wife, however, takes such matters much more seriously.

"Would you please call them back and just ask if it's a 'dress-up' breakfast," my wife asked, "and also find out if there will be a lot of people there, and maybe we can find out what they are wearing."

So I called the woman at the governor's office and was told that it was an informal breakfast and that it would probably be just the Voinoviches, the two of us, and a mutual friend. I reported back to my wife, who asked me what an "informal breakfast" meant.

"It probably means they'll have robes on over their pajamas," I joked. She didn't see the humor.

"You have got to find out what we are supposed to wear," she insisted.

So I called the governor's office again. "What should we wear to the breakfast with the governor?" I asked. I suspect the woman there was getting a little tired of my daily calls about the breakfast and replied, "Oh, just wear whatever you normally wear."

I interpreted that to be my daily attire of faded jeans, old shirt, sweater, and my favorite mustard-yellow jacket. I told Bonnie that the governor's office had said just wear whatever, that it was very informal. Furthermore, because we would be driving to Dayton to visit my daughter's family after breakfast at the statehouse, I suggested that traveling clothes would be just fine. With misgivings, Bonnie finally agreed.

On the morning of the breakfast, Bonnie put on a comfortable pair of slacks, some low shoes, and a sweatshirt that proclaimed "Ohio Is for the Birds," picturing some cardinals frolicking in the snow. We walked to the front door of the mansion and rang the doorbell.

The housekeeper opened the door and invited us in, just as a perfectly coiffed Janet Voinovich came down the stairs to meet us, wearing a smartly styled suit. My wife's eyes shot daggers at me. Janet seemed to take no notice of our attire and, giving each of us a hug, took us on a brief tour of the residence while we waited for the governor. Moments later my wife dug her fingernails into my hand as the governor joined us, dressed in a suit and tie. As we went into the dining room to sit down for breakfast, my wife whispered in my ear, "You're dead meat!"

Actually, it was a very enjoyable breakfast. George and Janet Voinovich treated us like old friends, and as we traded stories I think Bonnie forgot to be uncomfortable about our casual clothes. However, if we ever get invited to the White House, my wife assures me that *she* will decide what we wear for our visit, not me.

TOUR OF THE GOVERNOR'S RESIDENCE

While I can't guarantee that the governor's wife will personally conduct your tour, the official residence is open to groups for tours by reservation. Each Tuesday a member of the staff conducts tours of the lower floors of the 1920s-era mansion and the formal gardens behind the home. Every governor and his family since C. William O'Neil in the 1950s has lived here. All, that is, except James A. Rhodes, who chose to live in his own Columbus-area home. (He used the mansion only for formal entertainment.) You will get the opportunity to see, among other things, the silver service from the *U.S.S. Ohio*, on loan to the residence from the Ohio Historical Society, and the governor's personal office, where he often holds meetings with cabinet and staff members. In the summer you might even get a peek at the governor's personal vegetable garden, which he plants and tends all by himself. Tours are by reservation only.

Governor's Residence ☎ 614-644-7644
358 North Parkview Avenue • Bexley, Ohio 43209
Location: In Bexley, a suburb east of downtown Columbus.
Handicapped access: Some steps in house.

Governor's Residence. *Courtesy of the Governor's Office, State of Ohio.*

THE OHIO STATEHOUSE COMPLEX

Tours of the recently refurbished Ohio statehouse are given seven days a week. Here you can see where Abraham Lincoln's body lay in state in April 1865 when his funeral train paused in town. The rotunda has been restored to its former elegance, and you can peek in both chambers of the General Assembly, where Ohio's laws are enacted. Tours start about 9:00 a.m. and run throughout the day until about 3:00 p.m. Tours are free.

The Ohio Statehouse ☎ 614-752-6350
Broad Street · Columbus, Ohio 43215
Location: In the center of Columbus, Ohio.
Handicapped access: Yes.

Rhodes Tower Tours ☎ 614-466-7077
This is across the street from the statehouse and offers free tours of the Supreme Court.
Handicapped access: Yes.

Riffe Tower Tours ☎ 614-644-5250

This is a free tour of the General Assembly offices. It is also across the street from the statehouse.

Handicapped access: Yes.

Here are some more things to see and do while in Columbus.

AN ELECTRONICS OUTLET

This is one of six warehouses in the United States owned and operated by Radio Shack. Here they dispose of discontinued merchandise, warehouse-damaged items, and some "as is" stock—including one-of-a-kind items that may or may not work. Savings can range from forty to eighty percent. As for the warehouse-damaged stock, nothing is wrong with the merchandise, it's just the box that is damaged, so you get a savings and the same warranty that you would get on a new item right off the shelf. The merchandise is constantly changing, so there is no guarantee about what will be on sale. Inside the warehouse is also a regular Radio Shack store with regular merchandise.

Radio Shack Outlet ☎ 614-836-3060

4343 Williams Road • Groveport, Ohio 43125

Location: A suburb of Columbus on the Southeast side.

Handicapped access: Yes.

HENDERSON HOUSE BED AND BREAKFAST

This home was once an old farm, and there is a family legend that it was once owned by President Rutherford B. Hayes, although the Hayes Presidential Center in Fremont says it cannot substantiate this. The dining-room table once belonged to President Thomas Jefferson. In recent times many internationally known celebrities and politicians have stayed here, including boxing champ Archie Moore and the cast of *Phantom of the Opera*. Lee Henderson, the owner, is a former nationally known model, appearing in *Life Magazine* and *Playboy*. She says she is proud to be the first African-American operator of a bed and breakfast in Ohio—and is one of only nineteen in the Western Hemisphere. There are several rooms on the second floor, but only one has a private bath. The others share a bathroom on the first floor.

Henderson House Bed and Breakfast   ☎ 614-258-3463
1544 Atcheson • Columbus, Ohio 43203
Location: In Columbus, near downtown.
Handicapped access: Elevator to second floor.

The Muffins baseball team at Ohio Village. *Courtesy of Ohio Historical Society.*

THE ARCHIVE OF OHIO'S HISTORY

The Ohio Historical Society houses artifacts dating back to prehistoric times in Ohio; it also contains the state archives. The library is an invaluable resource for students, researchers, and writers. Next door is Ohio Village, a replica of a typical small Ohio community in the early nineteenth century. Costumed interpreters work as tinsmiths, cooks, bakers, and shopkeepers to bring that period alive to visitors. There is even a nineteenth-century baseball team that calls the village home and plays games, using rules from that era, with other classic teams from around the state. This is a way to learn about a lot of Ohio history in just one stop. Don't miss the bookstore in the museum; it contains many books on Ohio that are just not found in other bookstores.

Ohio Historical Society   ☎ 614-297-2439
Velma Ave. (17th Avenue and I-71) • Columbus, Ohio 43202
Location: On the north side of Columbus, visible from I-71.
Handicapped access: Yes.

AN UNUSUAL CAMERA SHOP

This shop has always been a personal favorite of mine, especially when I was taking a lot of pictures. Located in an old, abandoned church, the business was started by a group of Ohio State University students and advisors who were interested in photography. They began by buying out bankrupt camera stores, and also by picking up discontinued products and selling them by mail order out of one of the teachers' basements. The business grew to the extent that today it fills every nook and cranny of the old church. Much of the merchandise is old, some outdated and even rare. Prices are often negotiable, especially for the used merchandise and outdated film. This shop is a bit hard to find, but worth the effort. You can find photographic equipment here that cannot be located anywhere else.

Columbus Camera Shop   ☎ 614-267-0686
55 East Blake Street • Columbus, Ohio 43202
Location: On the north side of Columbus, near Ohio State University.
Handicapped access: Steps into building and onto second floor.

OHIO

63 Eugene Gets His Final Wish

I have this friend, Kevin Ruic. He used to run an airport but was afraid to fly. Well, that's not exactly true. He just didn't enjoy flying. Although he knew how to fly, he never bothered to get a license. Besides, he had all these good pilots that worked for him. Problem was, sometimes he had to fly. Like the day he discovered that he had booked a parachute jump and all of his pilots were gone. The customer, dressed as a chicken, was to jump near a stadium where a baseball game was going on, as a promotion for a restaurant.

When the parachutist (in his chicken costume) showed up, he informed Kevin that he needed to drop several thousand coupons over the stadium just before the game started.

Because no one else was available, Kevin decided to fly the parachutist himself. They took the door off a Cessna 206 and piled the bales of coupons in the back seat. The parachutist got in and Kevin took off.

It was a cloudy day: not a good one for parachuting. After circling the stadium several times, unable to see it because of low clouds, they decided that the next time they got a glimpse of it, they would make a pass over the parking lot and throw out the coupons.

Sure enough, a few minutes later there was a break in the clouds, and they spotted the stadium and parking lots. They banked the plane and circled to approach the parking lot, but by this time the clouds had closed in again. Approaching where he guessed the parking lot to be, Kevin yelled over the motor and wind noise to the parachutist, whose feathers were floating all over the cabin, "Throw out the coupons!"

"What?" the parachutist replied.

"Throw out the coupons, we're just about over the parking lot!" Kevin screamed, pointing down.

The chutist apparently misunderstood Kevin and thought he meant it was time to jump, so he did.

Just then the clouds parted again. Instead of being over the parking lot, he was over the stadium. The game was going on as the parachutist, dressed as a chicken, floated onto the playing field, stopping the action.

Kevin, banking the plane, reached back and tried to toss out the coupons. But it was taking too long to break open the bundles of coupons with just one hand and toss out a few at a time, and besides, they were plastering themselves all over the tail surface of his plane. So, Kevin reasoned, why not just toss out the bundles? When they hit the ground they would burst open, and the wind would spread them around for people to find when they returned to their cars. That's just what he did. What he didn't count on was the fact that the bricks of coupons weighed several pounds each and when they hit the cars in the parking lot, several windshields were cracked.

A couple of latecomers to the game had a narrow escape, crawling under a truck to escape the rain of blocks of chicken-restaurant coupons.

As luck would have it, an official from the Federal Aviation Administration was in the crowd at the stadium. He took down the number of the airplane and made several phone calls. It wasn't long after Kevin landed that a car with two FAA investigators pulled into his airport.

"Who was flying that plane this afternoon?" one of the agents asked, nodding to the airplane sitting outside the office, where Kevin had left it.

"I was," he replied truthfully.

"Do you realize that stunt you pulled over the baseball field this afternoon will probably result in a suspension of your pilot's license?" the government man said.

"Okay," said Kevin, "just as soon as I get one, I'll let you suspend it."

It wasn't that Kevin willfully set out to break the rules, he just hated to turn down any chance to make some money at his airport.

He received a phone call one morning.

"Do you dispose of cremains?" asked the voice of an elderly man.

"What do you mean?" asked Kevin.

"We have the ashes of a dead man whose last request was to have them spread over Lake Erie," responded the voice on the phone.

Kevin told the caller that for thirty-five dollars he could take care of the matter. The caller said he would be there in a short while.

Kevin gave little more thought to the matter until a gray-haired man stood before his operations desk, clutching a small cardboard box. The box, the man explained, contained the remains of his wife's former husband, Eugene, who had died some twenty-five years before. Eugene's last wish was to be cremated and to have his ashes spread on the waters of Sandusky Bay, where he had spent so many pleasant hours fishing. However, his widow had been so shaken with grief that she couldn't follow through. In fact, just the sight of the box of Eugene's ashes would set her off crying. She thrust the box at a neighbor and asked her to dispose of it. The neighbor, not understanding that the widow wanted Eugene's ashes spread on the lake, instead hid the box behind a chimney in the widow's house so that it was out of her sight. The widow, believing Eugene's last request had been met, finally overcame her grief and eventually married her present husband, with whom she had shared nearly twenty years. Now they were retiring and moving, and while cleaning out their home they discovered Eugene's ashes hidden behind the chimney in the attic.

Needless to say, the discovery had put a pall on their move, so the husband decided to take action himself by hiring Kevin to finally commit Eugene's ashes to the lake. Kevin asked if they wanted to accompany Eugene on his final flight, but the man said no and asked only that Eugene's ashes be disposed of in a tasteful way over the lake, as soon as was practical. He gave Kevin his thirty-five dollar fee and left the box of ashes on the counter.

Kevin swears that he had every intention of sending Eugene's ashes on a one-way trip on the very next flight he had scheduled over Sandusky Bay. Problem was, there just weren't many flights over the lake right then. And so Eugene became a fixture on the operations counter at the airport.

Many of the regulars at the airport came to include Eugene in their discussions, asking his advice or patting his cardboard box for luck. One fireman, who regularly walked his dog on the airport grounds at night, would stop by to pick up Eugene and take him along on the walk, talking to him. Close to the holidays, they even decorated Eugene's cardboard box with some tinsel. Eugene had become a regular at the airport. Kevin kept promising that at the first opportunity he was going to send Eugene on a flight over the lake, but he just never got around to it.

Finally, Kevin's chief pilot Frank O'Neil, a reverent man, had had enough. One stormy afternoon he sat staring at the box. Suddenly he grabbed Kevin and the box with Eugene's ashes and announced, "We are going to properly dispose of Eugene right now!"

"But it's raining," Kevin protested.

"It doesn't matter," said Frank. "It's a quiet day, and you haven't got any excuse. I'll fly, you bring Eugene."

A few minutes later, Frank, Kevin, and Eugene were flying towards Sandusky. The forecast had said the clouds had broken there; the area near the Lake Erie islands would be a perfect place to finally spread Eugene's remains.

But as they approached Sandusky Bay, the skies were not open, just gray and rainy. They were circling over the area, trying to figure out just where they were, when Kevin decided that one part of the lake was as good as another part, and so he pushed open the cockpit window, opened the box, and poured Eugene's ashes into the slipstream. Just as the last particles flew out the window, the clouds parted enough for Frank and Kevin to see that they were not over the bay but instead over downtown Sandusky. In fact, they had probably spread Eugene down the length of Washington Avenue.

But Kevin claims he did his job properly. There was a heavy rain that night and, he insists, by way of the storm sewers Eugene finally got his wish and ended up in Lake Erie.

THE FERRY TO KELLEYS ISLAND

There is almost year-round service to Kelleys Island. As long as the ice doesn't get too thick, the "BOB," or Big Orange Boat, as the locals call it, hauls both cars and people to the island. In the summertime, at the peak of tourist season, there is usually a boat coming or going about every thirty minutes. The number of boats drops when cold weather arrives, and when the ice gets solid, they stop altogether. Then the only way to the island is by airplane.

Kelleys Island Ferry Boat Service ☎ 419-798-9763
510 West Main Street • Marblehead, Ohio 43440
Location: The ferryboats leave from downtown Marblehead; watch for the signs.
Marblehead peninsula makes up one arm of the entrance to Sandusky Bay.
Handicapped access: Yes.

THE ISLAND-HOPPING FERRY

This boat carries only people, no cars. It runs in a circle from Port Clinton to South Bass Island and Kelleys Island. You can get off at any spot and jump back on when the next ferry arrives. They go continuously all day and into the evening. There is no additional charge if you want to stop at one of the islands and then rejoin the boat later. The boat also has a snack bar and bar on board and offers moonlight and sunset cruises.

The Island Hopper Ferry Boat ☎ 419-734-4336
4716 Karlite Drive • Port Clinton, Ohio 43452
Location: Get on Island Hopper at downtown Port Clinton dock, or main dock at
South Bass or Kelleys Island.
Handicapped access: Steps onto and in boat.

GUESTROOMS ON THE LAKEFRONT

This is a bed and breakfast with a lakefront view of Lake Erie that's like something out of a movie. The house was one of the big homes that once lined the downtown Kelleys Island waterfront, with a huge screened-in porch in front, where guests enjoy breakfast. There is also a garden in back of the home. It has been the scene of several weddings. Four guest rooms, shared bathrooms.

Crickett Lodge Bed and Breakfast ☎ 419-746-2263 or 216-842-4343
111 Lake Shore Drive • Kelleys Island, Ohio 43438
Location: On the lakefront on Kelleys Island.
Handicapped access: Steps into home; there are bedrooms on the first floor.

WHERE THE BUTTERFLIES ROAM

This new attraction on Kelleys Island is perhaps one of the strangest. It's a greenhouse where you go to watch butterflies! The owner has about two hundred butterflies in the greenhouse at all times. (Butterflies only live a few days after they hatch.) It's a rather peaceful way to spend an afternoon, sitting among flowers and fountains inside the greenhouse, while butterflies swoop and soar over your head, even landing on it once in a while. If you can't get enough at the greenhouse, they also sell butterfly cocoons that will, hopefully, hatch into your very own butterflies. There is also a gift shop that sells shirts, pictures, and other items adorned with (what else?) butterflies.

Butterfly Box Enterprises   ☎ 419-746-2454
604 Division Street • Kelleys Island, Ohio 43438
Location: Near downtown Kelleys Island on Lake Erie.
Handicapped access: Yes.

KELLEYS ISLAND WINE COMPANY

Winery owner Kurt Zettler's father was a retired diplomat when he decided to start a winery on the grounds of his favorite summertime vacation spot on Kelleys Island. The wines have become very successful, even winning some national awards for excellence. Today, Kurt and his wife, Robbie, not only offer wine tastings but also operate a delicatessen at the winery, offering imported cheeses and meats from around the world. They also welcome children, by providing them with a play area off the dining deck outside the winery.

Kelleys Island Wine Company   ☎ 419-746-2537
418 Woodford Road • Kelleys Island, Ohio 43438
Location: On Kelleys Island, ask anyone who lives on the island for directions. Chances are, if you take a bike or golf cart out for a ride, you'll pass the winery either coming or going.
Handicapped access: Steps into building.

THE WATER TAXI

If you stay too long at the winery, or anyplace else on the island (especially if you stay late into the night), you might find the ferryboats have stopped running for the day. What do you do if this happens, or if you have an emergency on the island and must get to the mainland right away? Not to worry. Ladd's Water Taxi has been carrying forgetful tourists back to their cars for years. They use speedy cabin cruisers and are on call twenty-four hours a day. This is a good number to tuck into your pocket before heading out for a day of fun on the islands.

Ladd's Water Taxi   ☎ 419-285-2571 or 419-285-2236
Ladd's Marina
229 Bayview • Put-in-Bay, South Bass Island, Ohio 43456
Location: Just call their office on Put-in-Bay, they will come to you.
Handicapped access: Steps into boat.

EMERALD EMPRESS

Here's a chance for a free boat ride on the biggest cruise boat in the Sandusky Bay area. The *Emerald Empress* can carry upwards of five hundred people on its three decks. It's also one of the newest cruise boats on the lake and offers daily cruises to the islands as well as special cruises for dinners and sunsets. On Sunday morning, if you can be at the dock by 7:00 a.m., you can get a free ride on the boat as it heads for Sandusky Bay, where church services are held on board.

Neuman Cruise and Ferry Line   ☎ 800-876-1907
101 E. Shoreline Drive • Sandusky, Ohio 44870
Location: The free ride is from their dock on the Sandusky, Ohio, waterfront each Sunday.
Handicapped access: Yes.

OHIO

64 Government Jeeps for One Cent?

We've all seen those advertisements. "Buy government surplus confiscated Rolls Royces for $10." Yeah, right! Usually it is a scam to get you to send in money for information that you can get from the government absolutely free. And, by the way, there are rarely government jeeps or confiscated luxury cars sold for a few dollars. If there were, you probably wouldn't want to buy them unless you had a truck to haul away the pieces.

In reality, the government disposes of equipment that has been deemed surplus in several ways: through sealed bids, at auctions, and at several "surplus stores." One of these is located at Wright Patterson Air Force Base in Dayton.

To reach the store, first you have to get a pass to enter WPAFB. You get that by going to gate 12A, the main gate. At the visitor center they will ask for a valid driver's license with your picture on it, and then give you a pass and a map to find the warehouse where the "store" is set up. It is open every Monday through Friday, from 10:00 a.m. until 3:00 p.m. and closed on weekends.

They accept only cash and major credit cards; absolutely no personal checks. The merchandise is sold as is, and there are no guarantees, warranties, or exchanges. Electrical merchandise may be plugged in to see if it works, but that's it. Once you pay for it, it's yours, forever. No returns.

The range of items for sale changes almost daily. What you will find at the Dayton location is mostly furniture, clothing, and office equipment. Cars, airplanes, and other large items are usually sold by bid or auction through the Battle Creek, Michigan, headquarters of the Defense Reutilization and Marketing Office.

The day I visited they were selling computers. The computers, mostly early IBM 8088 models, were going for one dollar each; black-and-white monitors were selling for as much as $25, if they worked. They also had brand-new nylon flying suits, still in their packaging, for $20 each (all size small). There were WWII flight goggles, in their original boxes, with extra plastic lenses, for one dollar. I noted that they were getting ready to sell off some office equipment. Locked file cabinets were expected to bring between $25 and $100. One man showed me a miniature tape recorder he had just purchased for $10. It worked. Remember: if you buy it, you can't return it. All sales are final.

Defense Reutilization and Marketing Office (DRMO)   ☎ 937-257-4203
Wright Patterson Air Force Base, Gate 12A • Dayton, Ohio
Location: Inside Wright Patterson Air Force Base, Dayton, Ohio.
Handicapped access: Yes.

HAMBURG WAGON

This is a Miamisburg institution. Since 1913, this tiny horse-drawn hamburger wagon has parked each day on Market Square. It's a very simple business. They cook small hamburgers, made from a secret recipe, in big iron skillets. That's all they sell: hamburgers. No cheeseburgers, no hot dogs; in fact, no soda pop or potato chips or french fries, either. They just sell hamburgers, usually by the bagful. And don't ask for catsup or mustard. They offer their hamburgers just four ways: with pickle, with pickle and onion, with onion, or with nothing. That's it. The lack of side dishes or drinks doesn't seem to deter customers who start lining up as soon as the wooden awning on the side of the wagon is lifted. The Hamburg Wagon is open every day from 11:00 a.m. until 8:00 p.m. They have no phone. By the way, just across the street is a small potato-chip factory where you can get a can of pop, as well as some fresh kettle-cooked chips.

Hamburg Wagon
Market Square • Miamisburg, Ohio
Location: Miamisburg is a suburb on the south side of Dayton.
Handicapped access: Yes.

A HANDS-ON MUSEUM

Dayton's Natural History Museum has been a longtime fixture in this town. They completed a new building in 1991 to house their collection, which includes a mummy and a skeleton of a woolly mammoth. It has also been home for many years to a small zoo. Most of the animals are indigenous to Ohio, and all are presented in glassed-in areas that closely resemble their natural habitat. They include turkey vultures, red foxes, snakes, and even some playful otters.

A new wing is about to be added that will include the local children's museum, which is moving. The new name of the complex will be the Dayton Museum of Discovery; it will be an intensely hands-on place that will encourage youngsters to touch, play, and experience many things. A temporary gallery now operating offers a canvas maze for youngsters to navigate, a play-store where little ones can take over the roles of shoppers and cashiers, and a giant sandbox to introduce kids to the science of archaeology.

Museum officials are predicting that when it is complete, it will rank with some of the major children's museums in the Midwest.

Dayton Museum of Discovery   ☎ 937-275-7431
2600 DeWeese Parkway • Dayton, Ohio 45414
Location: In a park on the northwest side of downtown Dayton.
Handicapped access: Yes.

A HORSE-DRAWN BOAT RIDE

The *General Harrison* is a seventy-foot-long replica of the type of canal boat that once plied the Miami Canal in southwestern Ohio. The Piqua Historical Area is a collection of original homes and a restored section of the old canal that ran nearby. Rides are available on the canal boat, which is pulled by horses and mules. The attraction is closed on Monday and Tuesday.

Piqua Historical Area   ☎ 937-773-2307 or 800-752-2619
9845 North Hardin Road • Piqua, Ohio 45356
Location: Piqua is about 25 miles of Dayton, Ohio, via I-75.
Handicapped access: Yes but limited; steps into boat, no wheelchairs.

OHIO

65 Marietta

One of the newest attractions in Marietta is a tour of sites where the Underground Railroad once ran. ("Underground Railroad" was the designation given to a series of safe hideaways and trails used by slaves escaping from what was then Virginia, directly across the Ohio River from Marietta.) The "conductors," as they were called, were people who guided the slaves across Ohio to the North, and freedom in Canada.

UNDERGROUND RAILROAD TOUR

This tour is conducted only for groups, and by reservation only. Local historian Henry Burke, whose ancestors were part of the Underground Railroad, leads the tours. He starts across the river in Williamstown, West Virginia. What many people forget is that prior to the Civil War the state of West Virginia did not exist. It was part of the state of Virginia, a slave-holding state. Still preserved on the West Virginia side of the river is Henderson Hall, a former plantation owned by the fifth generation of the Henderson family. The tour starts at the plantation with a viewing of the main house and some of the outbuildings built by slaves. The motorized trolley then carries you back on the Ohio side of the river. There are several stops in downtown Marietta to talk about hidden passages in old homes where escaped slaves were hidden. From there the tour heads north along the Muskingham River, which was used by escaping slaves as the main route to northern Ohio

This fascinating tour can also include a nighttime dinner cruise down the Ohio onboard the sternwheeler tour boat *Valley Gem*, where spotlights are used to point out coves along the riverbank where escaping slaves hide in the darkness of night.

The Levee House Restaurant ☎ 614-374-2233
127 Ohio Street • Marietta, Ohio 45750

Location: Marietta is on the banks of the Ohio River at the terminus of I-77 in Ohio.
Handicapped access: Steps onto trolley bus used in tour, steps at some stops.

A FORMER PLANTATION

This former slave-holding plantation offers tours from May until October. Hours change during the season, so call for times. The house is filled with original furniture, much of it made by slaves. On display are letters the family received from Confederate general Robert E. Lee and a letter from a slave who escaped from the family, made his way to Niagara Falls, Canada, and then wrote to Mr. Henderson asking if he could return. He did, only to stay a short while before leaving again.

Henderson Hall   ☎ 304-375-2129
WV Route 2, Box 103 • Williamstown, West Virginia 26187
Location: Directly across the Ohio River from Marietta, Ohio.
Handicapped access: No, steps throughout the home.

RIVERSIDE BED AND BREAKFAST

This historic home has stood on the riverbank of the Muskingham River in Marietta for more than a century. Alf and Dell Nicholas have converted it into a comfortable bed and breakfast, with private baths. A lovely New Orleans–type garden in the backyard has a gazebo and beautiful flowers. My favorite part is the hot tub that is available year round. The night I stayed here, the temperature outside was 20 degrees, yet I spent an enjoyable hour in 100-degree water in the hot tub watching the stars spread out over this confluence of the Muskingham and Ohio rivers. Sorry, no children allowed, and no pets or smoking, either.

Buckley House Bed and Breakfast   ☎ 614-373-3080
332 Front Street • Marietta, Ohio 45750
Location: On the main street, just north of downtown, along the Muskingham River.
Handicapped access: Steps to second floor.

A BIG COLLECTION OF TOY TRAINS

This is billed as one of America's most complete private collections of authentic toy electric trains. Its 1,500 feet of "O"-gauge track can operate up to fifteen trains at the same time. More than 250 vintage locomotives are on display. Trivia collectors please note: owner Jack Moberg, a retired dentist from Pennsylvania, used to be the next-door neighbor of TV's Mr. Rogers. He says that as boys they used to play with electric trains.

Harmar Station Historical Model Railroad Museum   ☎ 614-374-9995
Harmar Village
220 Gilman Street • Marietta, Ohio 45750
Location: Across Muskingham River from downtown Marietta.
Handicapped access: Yes.

Harmar Station Model Railroad Museum. *Courtesy of Harmar Station.*

OHIO

66 Sandusky Area

Two of the most frequently asked questions we get about northern Ohio are the following: "Where can I get a shore dinner?" and "Where is an inexpensive getaway close to home?" I found the answer to both of these questions in Sandusky.

ONE OF MY FAVORITE SHORE DINNERS

They must have the family of one of the area's last commercial fishermen working in the kitchen here. The Lake Erie perch and walleye are always fresh, never frozen. Now, this is not your white-tablecloth and crystal-stemware kind of restaurant. In fact, if you're a nonsmoker it can almost be disagreeable inside the tiny dining room because smokers seem to outnumber nonsmokers. The tableware is strictly plastic, with little packets of lemon juice and salt and pepper. There is no table service. You walk up to the counter and order what you want, or drive up to the window at the side of the building and pick up a carry-out order. But what you get is worth it. They sell fresh-cooked perch, either deep fried or broiled, by the pound. Be sure to have a bowl of their homemade turtle soup with your lunch. This is the kind of place where you'll find a lot of local residents, who really know their fish, stopping by for lunch and dinner. The service is quick and the food is good. What else do you need?

DeMore's Fish Den ☎ 419-626-8861
302 West Perkins Avenue • Sandusky, Ohio 44870
Location: On the south side of Sandusky.
Handicapped access: Yes.

BOWLING MEETS STAR WARS

Picture this: you've driven the family to Sandusky Bay for a week-long stay at Cedar Point, and it starts to rain. And rain. What do you do with the kids to keep them occupied and happy? This might be the answer: bowling. Star Lanes was one of the first bowling establishments to add lasers, smoke, and rock music to their bowling, called "Glow and Bowl." This gives the alleys a sort of Star Wars look as smoke pours across the lanes, interspersed with laser beams, all accompanied by the throbbing beat of heavy metal music. The owners say the kids love it, and they offer the show on some evenings and weekends. By the way, this is professional bowler Jeff Lizzi's home alley, and he is usually around to give some tips. Call for times when the "Glow and Bowl" is going on.

Sandusky Star Lanes, Inc.   ☎ 419-626-2413
2097 Cleveland Road · Sandusky, Ohio 44870
Location: On east side of Sandusky, not far from the Cedar Point entrance.
Handicapped access: Yes.

SLEEP INN

This is a relatively new motel, near the intersection of Ohio Route 2 and U.S. Route 250. It's located near the Sandusky Mall, just a short distance from the Cedar Point entrance, and close to all the attractions of Sandusky Bay. What they offer are some rooms that have gas fireplaces, king-sized beds, and whirlpool baths, all for a price lower than you might pay for a bed and breakfast in this area. They also throw in a free continental breakfast in their dining room, which has a fireplace. Add to this an indoor swimming pool and fitness room, and you get a fine place for a couples escape that's not far from home.

Sleep Inn   ☎ 888-927-5337 or 419-625-6989
5509 Milan Road (U.S. Route 250) · Sandusky, Ohio 44870
Location: On east side of Sandusky.
Handicapped access: Yes.

PARTY IN A BOXCAR

If you are looking for a spot to hold a family reunion, or an interesting place to take a scout group for an overnight trip, this might be just right. One of the smaller metroparks in Erie County, Coupling Reserve consists of just a train caboose, a boxcar, and a turn-of-the-century train station that has been converted into a party room, complete with living room with wood-burning fireplace, kitchen, and modern bathrooms. The park system will rent the cabooses and boxcars to groups to spend the night in. They have no heat, and no bathrooms, though there is electric light aboard the two railroad cars, and you get use of the station house that does have bathrooms, heat, and a place to cook your dinner and breakfast. The cars are rented by reservations only. Call first.

The Coupling Reserve   ☎ 419-625-7783
Erie County Metroparks
3910 East Perkins Avenue • Huron, Ohio 44839
Location: Between Huron and Milan, Ohio.
Handicapped access: Steps into the railroad cars.

Coupling Reserve. *Courtesy of Erie County Metroparks.*

NEW WAVE SNORKEL AND SCUBA CENTER

Now you may not think of Lake Erie as a place for diving or snorkeling, but all that has changed in the past few years, thanks, in part, to that pest, the zebra mussel. In many spots, the mussels have cleared the lake, and you can actually see the bottom on a clear, still day. This business near Port Clinton not only offers to teach you to dive and snorkel but will also lead you on dives to some of the many shipwrecks that dot the bottom of Lake Erie. We were taken to one in about forty feet of water just off the Lake Erie Islands. The sunken vessel could easily be seen in the water. In fact, using an underwater video camera, he shot pictures of fish and of the hulk on the bottom of the lake.

New Wave Snorkel and Scuba Center   ☎ 419-734-2240
1425 West Lakeshore Drive • Port Clinton, Ohio 43452
Location: Dive shop is on west side of Port Clinton.
Handicapped access: Steps into boat

SAILS OVER LAKE ERIE

If you have ever stood at the edge of Lake Erie as a storm approaches, watching sailboats hurrying for port, you know the awesome beauty that full sails against the dark clouds can create. Now there is a magnificent ship that can run before those storms, a ship that replicates the great wooden sailing freighters that once called Lake Erie home.

The *Red Witch* is a seventy-seven-foot-long schooner that flies 2,100 square feet of canvas from two tall wooden masts. Carrying forty-nine passengers and crew, she re-creates a nostalgic scene from a century ago when she rounds the Marblehead peninsula and sails past the lighthouse. The *Red Witch* carries a brass cannon, which is often fired in salute as she passes the Lake Erie landmark. Officially a Gaff Topsail Schooner, she was built in 1987 and saw service as a tour boat in Hawaii and San Diego before coming to her new home in Sandusky Bay. The ship, named for a John Wayne movie, *Wake of the Red Witch*, an epic sea story filmed in 1949, has become the only operating tall ship tour boat in Ohio.

The *Red Witch* offers two-hour cruises of Lake Erie, by reservation. Passengers are allowed to help the crew set the sails and even take the helm, if they wish. In 1997 the cost for a two-hour sail was eighteen dollars per person. There was a slightly higher charge to include a box lunch. Beer, wine, soda, coffee, and hot cider are available on board. Because this is a relatively new attraction, schedules may vary. Call for latest sailing information.

Red Witch Charter Company   ☎ 419-798-1244
P.O. Box 386 • Port Clinton, Ohio 43452
Location: Ship is based at Battery Park Marina, Sandusky, Ohio. Battery Park is located on the east side of the Sandusky waterfront.
Handicapped access: Steps onto boat, narrow aisles and steep steps on boat.

OHIO

67 The Sign of the Three Crosses

While driving on the highway, have you ever noticed, off in a field, three crosses—one golden and two blue? There is no sign, no advertisement, just three simple wooden crosses standing in a field. I have seen them in at least five states, but until recently had no idea what they were for or where they came from. The mystery has been solved.

A man by the name of Bernie Coffindaffer, from a small town in West Virginia, was responsible. A former Marine and self-made millionaire, he spent the last eleven years of his life traveling around the country putting up the crosses after, he said, receiving a visit from Jesus in the form of a vision. He said Jesus described the crosses to him and told him to go forth and build them. In those eleven years, from 1982 until his death in 1993, Bernie Coffindaffer placed the three crosses in twenty-nine states and even in the Philippines. He spent more than three million dollars, his retirement funds, and all of his savings to fulfill the vision. In all, he erected 1,800 cross clusters to stand as silent testimony to his vision. Eighty-nine of the locations are scattered across Ohio. He claimed he built the crosses to last at least thirty years. However, since his death, maintenance of the crosses has ceased, and already some are starting to fall into disrepair and many are disappearing from the landscape.

Location: One of the sets of crosses stands on the west side of Ohio Route 83, south of Wooster.

AN 1860S BED AND BREAKFAST

This is an excellent place to spend a night and also to learn more about Ohio's Amish lands. The red brick Italianate mansion was built in 1865, the year the Civil War ended. Today it is owned by journalists Al and Sue Gorisek. You may recognize Sue's name from the many stories she has written for *Ohio Magazine*. The bed and breakfast has six rooms with double beds, all with a private bath and air-conditioning. The furnishings reflect the Goriseks' love of antiques and range from Colonial to Victorian. The beauty of this spot is that the home is located only a block or so from downtown Loudonville, so it's an easy walk to several attractions. Rates are moderate. No smoking in the residence, and children are allowed only by prior arrangement. Open year round.

The Blackfork Inn   ☎ 419-994-3252
303 North Water Street • Loudonville, Ohio 44842
Location: In downtown Loudonville.
Handicapped access: Steps into home and to sleeping rooms.

BARGAINS AT THE GOLF BALL FACTORY

There are some good bargains here for golfers. Golf balls are made at an adjacent plant. While no tours of the plant are allowed, the factory store is open to the public. Here you will find discontinued products, overruns, and seconds (otherwise perfect golf balls with slight printing imperfections). They also sell other golf equipment, like clubs and clothes, at discounted prices. Savings of up to fifty percent are available on the golf balls. Open Monday through Saturday. Credit cards accepted.

Sunset Golf, Inc.   ☎ 419-994-5563
326 North Water Street • Loudonville, Ohio 44842
Location: Near downtown Loudonville, Ohio.
Handicapped access: Steps into building.

AN OLD-FASHIONED SODA FOUNTAIN

This is a place frozen in time. Sitting at the soda fountain makes you feel like it is 1950 again. But there is more. The shop also offers homemade candy and coffees from all over the world. For those of us who cannot tolerate sugar, there is a no-sugar-added ice cream with which they can make floats, so you can enjoy a fountain drink along with the rest of the family.

Village Pantry and Soda Shoppe   ☎ 419-994-4271
153 West Main Street · Loudonville, Ohio 44842
Location: Downtown Loudonville, Ohio.
Handicapped access: Yes.

HAMBURGERS AND SAUERBRATEN

A lot of local folks eat here. It's an authentic German restaurant with an American twist to its sandwiches—sauerbraten is served along with hamburgers. The bakery is what attracts many people. European pastries are made fresh each day. The owner, Karl Heinz, also makes his own breakfast cereal. It's very good!

Heinz Restaurant   ☎ 419-994-3646
146 North Water Street · Loudonville, Ohio 44842
Location: Next to police station, downtown Loudonville.
Handicapped access: Yes.

LOUDONVILLE CANOE LIVERY

Along with his family, my friend Dick Schafrath, former player with the Cleveland Browns and now a state senator, operates one of the larger canoe liveries in Loudonville. There are several places to rent canoes. All offer trips varying in length, from a couple of hours to adventures that go on for days. Dick's, like the others, has canoes, rafts, and kayaks, as well as large inner-tubes for those that want to spend a hot day just floating down the river. One reminder: always bring along some extra clothing. It's a rare visitor that takes a canoe ride and doesn't end up getting very wet.

Loudonville Canoe Livery   ☎ 419-994-4161
424 West Main Street · Loudonville, Ohio 44842
Location: On main street in downtown Loudonville.
Handicapped access: Yes to some boats.

OHIO

68 A Most Unusual Junction

Located not far from Roscoe Village, in Coshocton County, is a most unusual junction. Actually, the name of the place *is* Unusual Junction. It's just an old railroad station with several railroad cars, both passenger and freight, on the siding beside the building. It's what's inside that's so interesting.

When you walk through the front door, you may be met by owner Jerry McKenna, a transplanted Clevelander, playing a badly mangled trombone, badly. But he's not the attraction here. It's the thousands, and I do mean thousands, of bottles of hot sauce that fill the delicatessen in the front of the building. Everything from "Endorphin Sauce" to something labeled "XXXX Double Atomic." Jerry, you see, specializes in having some of the hottest hot sauces in the world. But that's not the only attraction here. Just behind the aisles and aisles of hot sauce is Jerry's bridal shop!

That's right, bridal shop. Now to you and me it may seem a strange mixture of businesses—hot sauce, deli items, bridal gowns and veils. Jerry says it just makes sense. He points out that brides-to-be are often accompanied by male members of the wedding party, like father, brothers, ushers, and even, sometimes, the prospective bridegroom. So while the women are trying on dresses, the men tend to drift towards the front of the store to look over the hot sauces. Some end up buying several. And, if it's a particularly long fitting, Jerry may even sell sandwiches and ice cream to the bridal party.

Now Jerry admits that some people are slightly taken aback when they first enter his shop, but he says by the time they leave they are usually chewing on a sandwich and packing a couple of bottles of "Louisiana Sunshine" into the bag with the bridal veil.

Unusual Junction is open seven days a week. In the summertime there are crafts in some of the railway cars. A courtyard is being built beside the station for bridal showers.

Unusual Junction Bridals and Delicatessen
☎ 614-545-6007 or 800-532-8948
56310 U.S. Route 36 • West Lafayette, Ohio 43845
Location: On U.S. Route 36 east of Coshocton.
Handicapped access: Yes.

SALT FORK STATE PARK

Ohio's largest state park like other state parks offers both a lodge and cabins. There is also a marina, and indoor and outdoor swimming pools. If you like wildlife, just take a drive through the grounds on a warm night. Deer wander in herds everywhere here. It's not unusual to find several standing on the front porch of the lodge. If you do drive in the park at night, be extremely careful; the deer do not stop and look before dashing across a road. At the marina you can rent boats and skidoos.

Salt Fork State Park   ☎ 800-282-7275
Box 672 • Cambridge, Ohio 43725
Location: Just north and east of I-77 and I-70 at Cambridge, Ohio.
Handicapped access: Yes.

OHIO-MADE LAWN ORNAMENTS

This is a good spot to pick up some Ohio-made pottery and cement lawn ornaments. You can find lots of seconds from some of the famous Ohio pottery names and save up to fifty percent (or more) on things like birdbaths, garden globes, and huge crocks— even cement cows, pigs, and geese that can be dressed in clothes. You could probably save a few more cents by going direct to the factories to buy some of these things, but here you can get a good variety, save a lot of money in gas and wear and tear on your car, and save time.

Ohio Pottery   ☎ 614-872-3137
Exit 164 at I-70 • Norwich, Ohio 43767
Location: On I-70 west of Cambridge.
Handicapped access: Gravel drive, but everything on one floor with wide doors and aisles.

BLOOMER'S CANDY

This is one of the big names in candy in central Ohio. Bloomer's chocolates are sold at many small markets and specialty stores. While tours of their factory are not available, there is a quaint factory store in the local railroad station. The advantage of going to a factory store is obvious: you get a choice of all of the many varieties they make. The candy is usually fresher, too, and sometimes seconds are available at discounted prices.

The Sweet Station (Bloomer's Candy) ☎ 614-455-2314
231 Market Street • Zanesville, Ohio 43701
Location: In downtown Zanesville, Ohio.
Handicapped access: Yes.

MICHIGAN

69 Clumsy? Who's Clumsy?

I have always been identified with Gerald Ford. Not because of my politics, but because he and I suffer from the same malady: clumsiness.

For example, when Mr. Ford was still in office he came to Cleveland, and I was assigned to do what is called a "one-on-one" interview. In other words, I was the only reporter in the room asking questions of him. My camera crew and I arrived at his hotel suite at the appointed hour, and we were ushered into the parlor, where a gaggle of local officials and Secret Service agents were milling around. In the center of the room was the president. A press aide escorted me across the room and introduced me to Mr. Ford. As he turned towards me to shake hands, I stepped forward, misjudging the distance, and immediately stepped on his foot! Now consider how you would feel if you accidentally stepped on the foot of the president of the United States. I was terribly embarrassed, but Mr. Ford was very gracious, and, wincing a bit, waved off my apologies and limped to a nearby easy chair that my videographer, Cook Goodwin, had moved to a position near the center of the room.

The press aide indicated we would have only a few minutes for the interview and emphasized that we should hurry with our preparations.

While Cook set up the tripod for the camera, I grabbed one of our tall light stands and walked quickly behind Mr. Ford to set up the light. As I ran the cord over to a wall outlet, I did not notice that it was wrapped about the light-stand legs! It was the shout from an alert Secret Service agent that alerted me; he caught the light as it toppled over, nearly striking the president.

I got several glares from agents. Cook took over the setting up of the lights while I seated myself across from Mr. Ford, stammering yet another apology for my clumsiness.

Again Mr. Ford was gracious enough to wave off my apologies, and we launched into the interview. I remember very little of what I asked him, other than that some of his answers were rather long and we changed film at least once before his press aide indicated our time was up.

As I stood to say good-bye to the president, I realized that both of my feet had gone to sleep—I had no feeling in either one. As I tried to step forward to shake hands with the still-sitting Mr. Ford, I stumbled and fell to my knees, my head landing in the president's lap. Mr. Ford said nothing for a moment as startled agents reached to pull me up. As they lifted me to my feet, the president looked intently at me and said, "Young man, by any chance do you vote Democratic?"

Mr. Ford was retired when our paths almost crossed again. I went to Grand Rapids, Michigan, Mr. Ford's hometown, to visit the Ford Presidential Library. This beautiful edifice contains not only many momentos of his career in Congress and the Presidency but also a personal office that he uses when he visits Grand Rapids. It just so happened that the day we were slated to do a One Tank Trip to Grand Rapids, Mr. Ford was also in town to give a speech that evening and was expected in the library sometime that afternoon to do some work in his office. Museum officials were glad to have us there to do a story on their facility, but were understandably distracted by the presence of Secret Service agents, who were checking out the building. They indicated that we could wander through the museum on our own while they escorted the agents on the upper-floor security check.

We had been videotaping for about fifteen minutes when we came to the centerpiece of the museum, an exact replica of the presidential oval office, just as it was in the White House when Mr. Ford was president. Velvet ropes blocked entrance through each doorway. Videographer Bill West and I stood there looking, Bill taking some shots of the presidential desk and chair through the doorway. I turned to Bill and said, "I wonder what it would feel like to sit behind that desk."

"Don't do it," warned West. But I already had unhooked the velvet rope and was walking across the room towards the chair.

I pulled it out and had just settled into it, waiting for West to focus his camera on me, when Gerald Ford's voice boomed through the room: "This was the desk and chair that I used as president of the United States."

I leapt, red-faced, from the seat, believing I had just been caught by the former president.

But no one was there. There was just the sound of the running feet of the security guards. I had tripped an electronic beam that turned on a recording of Mr. Ford's voice and also alerted guards that someone was inside the exhibit, where they were not supposed to be.

Museum officials, although polite, were not happy with me, and for the rest of our short visit, we had an escort. If you get to Grand Rapids be sure to see the Ford Presidential Museum, but *don't* try to sit in Mr. Ford's chair.

GERALD R. FORD PRESIDENTIAL MUSEUM

Gerald R. Ford was the only American who ever served as both vice president and president of the United States without having been elected by the American people. The momentos of his administration are housed here in Michigan in a beautiful building not far from where he started his political career in the late 1940s. There is a replica of the president's White House oval office, and Mr. Ford also has an office located inside the museum for his personal use when he visits Grand Rapids. In the gift shop you can buy a golf ball autographed by Mr. Ford and presidential cufflinks. There is an admission charge, but children under the age of fifteen are admitted free.

Gerald R. Ford Presidential Museum   ☎ 616-451-9263
303 Pearl Street, Northwest • Grand Rapids, Michigan 49504-5353
Location: In downtown Grand Rapids, Michigan. About a four-hour drive from northern Ohio.
Handicapped access: Yes.

AVIATION HISTORY BROUGHT TO LIFE

One of best aviation museums in the Midwest is located not far from Grand Rapids. More than forty airplanes are on display here;

they range from a replica of the Wright brothers' first commercial airplane to late-model jet fighters. The best thing about this museum is that these planes still fly! In the summer, weather permitting, yet another antique aircraft takes to the sky, so visitors can see how these craft looked in their true element. Also—and again, weather permitting—you can take a ride in a historic Ford Tri-Motor, the world's first airliner, owned by the museum. (There is an extra cost for this in addition to the admission for the museum.) Youngsters of any age can try nearly a dozen flight simulators, ranging from the Link Trainer of World War II to a modern simulator that takes you for a ride in a World War II Navy Corsair fighter plane. This is one museum the kids are gonna love!

Kalamazoo Air Museum (Kal Air Zoo)   ☎ 616-382-6555
3101 East Milham Road • Kalamazoo, Michigan 49007
Location: Kalamazoo is in western Lower Michigan, about a four-hour drive from Northeast Ohio.
Handicapped access: Yes.

Ford Tri-Motor, Kalamazoo Air Zoo. *Courtesy of Kalzoo Air Museum.*

A SPECTACULAR ELECTRIC TRAIN DISPLAY

I've seen a lot of electric train displays, but this is truly one of the most spectacular. Owner Seth Geim has devoted much of his life to building this display in the upper floor of his family's former cow barn. The star of the attraction is his one-of-a-kind replica of the Royal Gorge in Colorado, with a scale model of the suspension bridge that carries trains over the gorge. He had to build a new two-story addition on the barn to accommodate the twelve-foot-deep canyon and river. The exhibit fills 2,800 square feet of the barn and is open to the public every Saturday. Geim operates a train shop on the first floor that is open Tuesday through Saturday. He will open the train exhibit to groups by special reservation.

The Train Barn Hobby Shop and Museum   ☎ 616-327-4016
10234 East Shore Drive • Kalamazoo, Michigan 49002
Location: This one is a bit difficult to locate. It is actually in Portage, Michigan, a suburb of Kalamazoo. When calling for reservations, ask for directions and map.
Handicapped access: Steps to second-floor attraction.

STUART AVENUE INN

This inn is located just blocks from downtown Kalamazoo and is made up of several historic homes, one of them a mansion formerly owned by the Upjohn pharmaceutical family. The homes, while maintaining a Victorian atmosphere, are modernized with private baths, air-conditioning, gas log fireplaces, and large whirlpool tubs in some rooms. There are small kitchens in some of the rooms. The gardens surrounding the inn are beautiful and include a gazebo, pool, and a large lawn. Rates range from $60 to $150 a night and include a rather large continental breakfast the next morning.

Stuart Avenue Inn   ☎ 616-342-0230
229 Stuart Avenue • Kalamazoo, Michigan 49007
Location: Near downtown Kalamazoo. Ask for directions when making reservations.
Handicapped access: Yes, to some rooms.

A MUSEUM FOR PEOPLE WHO LIKE TECHNOLOGY

This is another good museum for youngsters. Just about everything in it is interactive. Completed in 1996, it features cutting-edge technology, including a machine that can create a tornado and a giant robot that interacts with the audience while teaching about space, computers, and the like. Best of all, this museum was selected by the families who lost loved ones in the *Challenger* space shuttle disaster to be one of the *Challenger* space learning centers. Students and their teachers come here to spend a day in a simulated mission to a space station, the students taking the roles of astronauts and scientists. Kids seem to really get into it and love the experience. In the summer a shorter version is held for other visitors. Admission to the museum is free, but there is a charge for some of the programs.

Kalamazoo Valley Museum   ☎ 616-373-7990
230 North Rose Street · Kalamazoo, Michigan 49007
Location: In downtown Kalamazoo.
Handicapped Access: Yes.

MICHIGAN

70 Meechigan!

I spent a week in Michigan recently and, despite the fact that I never could learn to say "Meechigan" properly, I had a great time. We visited a tall ship that doubles as a bed and breakfast and saw a replica of the Austrian chapel where the immortal hymn "Silent Night" was written. Michigan is right next door and offers a whole list of attractions that we don't have in Ohio.

RAISE THE SAILS ON A TALL SHIP

This 100-foot-long authentic tall ship sails from Traverse Bay daily on a two-hour cruise. Visitors who wish to can help raise the sails and become, temporarily, members of the crew. It's a beautiful sight on a windy day as the ship leans into the wind. The best part comes at the end of the cruise; visitors may, while the ship is docked, spend the night aboard, sleeping in private rooms and in the morning having breakfast with the crew. If you want more adventure, the *Malabar* has a sister ship named the *Manitou*, also over 100 feet in length, that offers three- to six-day cruises of the Traverse Bay and Lake Michigan shoreline. You sail all day and then dock at one of the islands or along the coast somewhere for a night's sleep, and then resume your journey the next day. All the sailing is done in daylight so you don't miss anything while sleeping.

The Tall Ship *Malabar* ☎ 800-872-8377 or 616-947-1120
13390 South West Bay Shore Drive, Box 8 • Traverse City, Michigan 49684
Location: Traverse Bay is in the northwest corner of lower Michigan.
Handicapped access: Steps on ship, narrow aisles, steps into cabins.

RIDE THE DUNES

This is one of three places left where you can ride over the sand dunes along the edge of Lake Michigan. Some of the dunes rise a hundred feet or more into the sky, making veritable mountains of sand, literally burying anything in their way. The dunes are alive, meaning that the wind moves and reshapes them year after year. At times, while riding over these dunes, you might think you were in the middle of the Sahara Desert. You can see nothing but sand dunes in every direction. The trip across the dunes is made in specially built four-wheel-drive trucks that race down hills and run along the edge of the lake, splashing through waves, and then back up the hill and over the dunes again. It's an exciting ride and one that will someday no longer be allowed, because of the threat to the environment.

Mac Woods Dune Rides ☎ 616-873-2817
Box 251 • Mears, Michigan 49436
Location: Just north of Muskegon, Michigan, on the shores of Lake Michigan.
Handicapped access: Steps into truck.

Mac Woods Dune Rides..

THE LARGEST CHRISTMAS STORE

The world's largest Christmas store is larger than four football fields! It contains over 50,000 gifts and trimming from around the world and is open year round. In the parking lot is an exact replica of the tiny chapel in Oberendorf, Austria, where the beloved hymn "Silent Night" was first sung on Christmas Eve in 1818. On the chapel grounds are plaques with the first verse of "Silent Night" printed in more than three hundred languages.

Bronner's Christmas Wonderland   ☎ 800 ALL-YEAR or 517-652-9931
25 Christmas Lane • Frankenmuth, Michigan 48734
Location: Frankenmuth is north of Flint, Michigan.
Handicapped access: Yes.

BAVARIA IN MICHIGAN

Blink your eyes and you'll think you are walking down the street in a Bavarian village. Flowerpots hang from every lamppost, most of the buildings sport a Bavarian facade, and the sound of polka music is everywhere. A clock shop is built to resemble a three-story cuckoo clock. There are horse-drawn carriage rides, riverboat rides on a sternwheeler, and covered bridges that lead to a hotel resembling a Bavarian castle. This is the only community in the United States where one of the instruments played in the high-school marching band is a twenty-foot-long Alpine horn.

Frankenmuth Convention and Visitors Bureau
☎ 800-FUN-TOWN or 517-652-8668
635 South Main Street • Frankenmuth, Michigan 48734
Location: Frankenmuth is north of Flint, Michigan.
Handicapped access: Yes to many of the businesses.

MICHIGAN

71 Tubas and Butterflies

We made a trip to Lansing, Michigan, recently to see what I consider one of the world's most unusual museums. It honors the tuba. Best of all, it's located in a restaurant, where you can eat while listening to a tuba serenade. It doesn't get much better than that!

THE TUBA MUSEUM (AND RESTAURANT)

One of the club's owners plays the tuba. He was always forgetting to take it home after working all day in the restaurant, so his partner took to hanging the tuba on the wall to keep it out of the way. Well, wouldn't you know, someone came in, saw the tuba hanging on the wall, thought the restaurant collected tubas, and brought in an old one from home. The collection began to grow, and today the walls are covered with tubas—from large "raincatchers" to a double-bell euphonium. Most of them still work, too. People who play the tuba have been known to drive hundreds of miles out of their way to visit the world's only tuba museum (and also to get a free beer or ice-cream cone by unlimbering their tubas and playing a tune for the folks eating in the restaurant).

As for the restaurant, just like the name says, its cuisine is international. Might be South American today, Chinese tomorrow, Italian the next. The owners have traveled all over the world and bring recipes from everywhere together in their restaurant. The menu has twenty-two pages! Open seven days a week for lunch and dinner. A fun place.

Traveler's Club Int'l Restaurant & Tuba Museum   ☎ 517-349-1701
2138 Hamilton Road • Okemos, Michigan
Location: Okemos is a suburb of Lansing, Michigan.
Handicapped access: Steps into restaurant and narrow bathroom aisles.

BUTTERFLY HOUSE

The Botany department here at Michigan State University has become a tourist attraction. A greenhouse filled with succulent plants is also filled with hundreds of butterflies, who have become so used to humans that they land on heads and hands. It's a pleasant, quiet way to spend an hour, sitting among and admiring the butterflies.

Open seven days a week. There is no admission, but donations are accepted.

Botany Department, Michigan State University ☎ 517-355-0229
East Circle Drive, Michigan State University • Lansing, Michigan 48824-1312
Handicapped access: Steps in part of the building.

DUSTY'S ENGLISH INN

This is where the governor of Michigan almost got to live, and now you can stop in for a night. When plans to buy this beautiful English Tudor estate for the governor's official residence fell through, the retired president of United Press International's radio division decided to buy it and convert it into an inn. It looked a lot like some of the estates in England that he had grown to love while assigned there. Today there are eleven rooms, all with private baths. The first floor is given over to a formal restaurant that has become a favorite for local folks on special occasions. A full English breakfast is served to overnight guests.

Dusty's English Inn ☎ 800-858-0598 or 517-663-2500
728 South Michigan Road • Eaton Rapids, Michigan
Location: Eaton Rapids is a suburb of Lansing, Michigan.
Handicapped access: Steps to some rooms, and narrow doorways to bathrooms.

INDIANA

72 A Toll Taker with a Sense of Humor

Have you ever noticed that some of the attendants in the booths along toll roads seem rather surly? Well, disinterested perhaps. The best examples are the ones working on the New York Turnpike. I have yet to have one of them smile at me or even say "Have a nice day" as they take my money. In fact, they usually have a set of stereo headphones on and are oblivious to the fact that I am sitting beside their open door until I proffer money, which they automatically snatch from my hand, tossing back change and mumbling "Car waitin' behind you, please count your change somewhere else." For the last eighteen years, I have had sort of a contest with many of the photographers I have worked with. When we approach the New York Turnpike, we smile and say to the toll taker "Good day, sir! How are you?" So far not one has responded. It is always the same. A hand shoots out and a mechanical voice says, "That'll be three dollars and eighty-five cents."

Perhaps they dislike their jobs. I can understand the boredom of standing hour after hour, receiving money from strangers in cars. Then of course there are the inane questions from people who say they are lost. Being expected to be a font of information about local hotels and eating places, a stand-in for the local tourist industry. . . I mean, the nerve of some people. To expect a toll collector who is paid with public money to be courteous to the public? The very idea!

In fairness to the tollbooth workers of the Ohio Turnpike, I must say I have never run into this problem in Ohio. Ohio toll collectors are usually polite and helpful if you have a question.

But my favorite toll takers are the ones on the Indiana Turnpike. Indiana toll collectors are never too busy to say hello or wish you a good day. They almost rush out of their booths to shout "Welcome to Indiana!" I am often struck by the thought that perhaps they are paid a bonus for each motorist who stays in the state overnight.

The lengths they will go to to entertain are legend. Videographer Cragg Eichmann and I had a recent assignment in South Bend,

Indiana. It had been a tiring five-hour drive from Cleveland, and when we reached the tollbooth there was a line of cars ahead of us and behind. I groaned. We were just on schedule for an appointment at the new College Football Hall of Fame, and if we sat in line here we were going to be late.

As we inched forward, I could see the toll collector having an animated conversation with each customer. When it was finally our turn, he met us with a large smile.

"Good morning, gentlemen, how are we today?" he said with such earnestness that we felt compelled to reply. "Did you have a good trip...?" he inquired as he made change from a ten-dollar bill.

We replied that we did and that we were in a bit of a hurry to get to the College Football Hall of Fame, and could he point out the quickest route.

His face fell. The smile was replaced by a look of compassion. "I could tell you," he said somberly, "but it won't do you much good. The place burned down last night."

We were shocked. We had driven five hours to do a story that had just gone up in flames!

"What happened?" I blurted out, ignoring the honking of impatient motorists behind us.

"Some problem with the boiler, I think," he said. A smile was starting to creep back onto his face.

"What are we gonna do now?" Eichmann asked me.

"By the way," the toll taker interjected, "I was just kidding. It didn't burn down, I just wanted to see if you were paying attention."

"You're not kidding now, are you?" I implored, feeling a sense of relief sweep over me.

"Naw, I just like to pull people's chains now and then, it makes the day go quicker," he answered as he motioned us away and towards South Bend, ready for his next victim.

Hoosiers! Go figure...!

THE NEW HOME OF COLLEGE FOOTBALL LEGENDS

This attraction once called Ohio home. In fact, it was at the entrance to King's Island Amusement Park, near Cincinnati. Too much competition from the amusement park caused the Hall of Fame officials to decide to move it to another city. South Bend had the highest bid. They have spent millions of dollars on the new home for the Hall of Fame, which now includes a state-of-the-art computer display that lets you call up any player ever named to the hall. You can see not only a picture of the player, but also his career record, and, in many cases, you can see him in action in his heyday by way of film and videotape. Lots of interactive things to do here. You can try kicking a field goal, make a touchdown run through linebacking dummies, or play quarterback and see if you can pass the ball for a touchdown. By way of videotape, you can even join sportscaster Chris Shenkel in the play-by-play announcing booth and call a few plays yourself. This is a fun place with something for everyone in the family.

College Football Hall of Fame   ☎ 219-235-9999
111 South St. Joseph Street • South Bend, Indiana 46601
Location: Right in downtown South Bend, near the St. Joseph River.
Handicapped access: Yes.

BEARCREEK FARMS RESORT AND INN

This started out as a getaway for an Indiana restaurant owner. He began adding things to his own farm retreat and eventually created a farm resort. The motel cabins look like miniature farmhouses. There is a theater with live entertainment, including some guest visits by big-name entertainers. There are several restaurants on the property, shops where candy and crafts are sold, a museum, and even a miniature train. Prices are reasonable and some great off-season savings packages include motel room, dinner, and theater tickets. One problem: this place is located far out in the boondocks, and you will need a map to get there.

Bearcreek Farms Resort and Inn   ☎ 800-288-7630 or 219-997-6822
R.R. 1, PO Box 180B • Bryant, Indiana 47326
Location: Just across Indiana border, near St. Marys and Celina, Ohio.
Handicapped access: Yes.

AUBURN-CORD-DUESENBERG MUSEUM

This was once the home of these great automobiles, and the 1930s showroom in the front of the factory has been restored to the elegance of that early automobile era. Many of the Cords, Auburn Boatails, and Duesenbergs are on display, as well as a good assortment of other automobiles that once sped down the highways of

America. One of the great auto shows is held here each year; it brings classic car lovers from all over the country. Be sure to make hotel reservations early. The ACD Museum is open seven days a week.

Auburn-Cord-Duesenberg Museum   ☎ 219-925-1444
1600 South Wayne Street • Auburn, Indiana 46706
Location: On I-69 south of the Indiana Turnpike not far from Fort Wayne, Indiana.
Handicapped access: Yes.

WHERE EVERYONE LIKES DAN QUAYLE

Dan Quayle, vice president of the United States during the George Bush administration, grew up in this town, and the local folks love him. They have turned a former church into a museum that has in its collection his report cards, his golf sweater, even his elementary-school lunch box. On Quayle's insistence, the local folks dedicated a portion of the building as a memorial to every person who has ever served as U.S. vice president. My favorite exhibit was a gift from a Texas woman. When officials received it, they weren't sure where to put it. They finally mounted it in the men's bathroom. It's a bronze plaque that says "I may not have known John F. Kennedy, but I was vice president of the United States." The plaque is obviously a reference to Lloyd Bentsen's famous dig at Quayle in the 1988 vice-presidential debate ("I knew John F. Kennedy...you are no John Kennedy").

Dan Quayle Center and Museum   ☎ 219-356-6356
815 Warren • Huntington, Indiana 46750
Location: Huntington is off U.S. Route 224 near Fort Wayne, Indiana.
Handicapped access: Yes.

DAN QUAYLE'S FAVORITE RESTAURANT

If you are a real fan of Dan Quayle's, you can stop at his favorite eating spot in town, Nick's. Although they sell a Quayleburger, employees admit Quayle rarely orders one. He likes the veal cutlet and the raspberry pie.

Nick's Kitchen   ☎ 219-356-6618
506 North Jefferson Street • Huntington, Indiana 46750
Location: Just down North Jefferson, two blocks from the museum.
Handicapped access: Narrow aisles, step into restaurant.

PENNSYLVANIA

73 Where the Ducks Walk on the Fish

I have always been fascinated by oddball tourist attractions. You know, the place whose claim to fame is the largest ball of string in the world, or the world's largest collection of false teeth. I don't know why such places call to me, but they do, and I have discovered that a lot of other people also find such destinations irresistible. One of my favorites is just over the edge of Ohio in Pennsylvania. It's a place where the ducks walk on the fish.

Pymatuning Lake, which is partly in Ohio and partly in Pennsylvania, was created out of old kettle ponds and a marsh in the 1930s. The dam spillway is near Linesville, Pennsylvania. Someone in the early 1930s noticed that fish, mostly carp, would gather at the spillway to take advantage of the dead bugs and other flotsam gathered by the running water and washed over the dam. Probably one of the early fishermen, who was having lunch while looking at the spillway, tossed a crust from a sandwich into the water. Much to his surprise the water exploded in a mass of roiling carp, all fighting for the bread crust. Amused by the sight, he may have thrown his entire sandwich, bit by bit, into the water. By now he had attracted nearby wild ducks, who, also trying to get the bread, started walking across the top of the surging mass of fish. Suddenly a tourist attraction was born.

The first trip that I can remember taking with my family was on a spring day in the late 1930s, when we drove from Henrietta, Ohio, to Pymatuning Lake to see for ourselves the spot where the ducks could walk on the backs of the fish. I remember the number of little stands selling loaves of stale bread to the tourists to use to feed the fish. Now, more than a half century later, the fish-feeding still goes on.

Now you might not think that feeding fish is a very interesting thing to do, but just travel to the Linesville spillway on a pleasant summer day, and you will see cars from every state parked in the lakeside parking lot. The souvenir stand does a big business in T-shirts, hot dogs, and, of course, stale bread, which recently sold at three loaves for a dollar. The carp have grown considerably from their starchy diet over the years, and it is not uncommon to see fish as long as thirty inches. Hundreds, perhaps thousands of them swarm like bees when a piece of bread comes sailing into the water from the two feeding stations that have been built near the spillway. People are quick to tell you that fish-feeding at Pymatuning has become a family tradition, going back generations. Indeed, my son and two daughters are the third generation of my family to take part in the ritual.

When you stand at the edge of the spillway and look down on the roiling mass of fish, all with their mouths opened, you can't help but wonder what would happen if a human fell into that mass. Would they be instantly devoured, like in the movies when someone falls into a river filled with piranhas? I put that question to a man operating the souvenir stand. He admitted that the only person he knew that had ever fallen in was himself! He told me that he was walking along the edge of the lake, near the spillway, cleaning up empty bread wrappers dropped there by careless tourists when he stepped on a slippery spot and went headfirst into the lake. He said he, too, had often wondered what the fish would do if presented with a human instead of bread for their free meal. His sudden entry into the lake apparently startled the fish, who darted away, and he scampered out of the water before they got curious enough to return. He suspects that his large size would have kept the fish away in any event, but he didn't want to go back into the water to test his theory.

LINESVILLE SPILLWAY

Bring your own bread, rolls, or whatever. If you don't, there are bread stands along the road leading to the spillway, and bread can be purchased at the souvenir stand. Admission is free and there are restrooms at the parking lot. There are two areas for feeding the fish: one directly above the spillway and another directly off the parking lot.

Linesville Spillway
Pymatuning Lake · Linesville, Pennsylvania
Location: Linesville is on U.S. Route 6, just across the Ohio line in Pennsylvania.
Handicapped access: Yes.

PYMATUNING STATE PARK CABINS

These cabins, located on the Pennsylvania side of Pymatuning Lake, sleep six people and are relatively new. They offer heat and running water and are equipped with beds, furniture, and a kitchen. Just bring your own bedding and food. Some of the cabins are located on the edge of the lake. They are just a short distance from the Linesville Spillway. Boat rentals and snowmobile trails are offered in the park.

Pymatuning State Park Cabins   ☎ 412-932-3141
Jamestown, Pennsylvania 16134
Location: On the eastern side of Pymatuning Lake.
Handicapped access: Yes, to some cabins.

PYMATUNING STATE PARK (OHIO)

If you would rather stay on the Ohio side, try the cabins at the Pymatuning State Park. They have recently been refurbished with gas fireplaces and color televisions with cable. They also offer running water, bathrooms, and kitchens. All you need to bring is bedding and food. You can rent by the night during off season. The park also offers swimming, boating, and fishing.

Pymatuning State Park   ☎ 216-293-6329
P.O. Box 1000 · Andover, Ohio 44003
Location: On the western side of Pymatuning Lake.
Handicapped access: Yes.

PENNSYLVANIA

74 Wings Are Not Just for Buffalo

Some of the very best Buffalo Wings in the country can be found right next door in Pennsylvania, in a complex of three restaurants: the Hot Rod Cafe, Tulley's, and the Quaker Steak and Lube. The former gasoline station has gained much attention for its preparation of Buffalo Hot Wings. In fact, they have been proclaimed to have the "Best Wings in the U.S.A." in a contest held in Cleveland and have won several other competitions in Ohio, Pennsylvania, and other states. They even went so far as to go to Buffalo, New York, and take on the Anchor Bar, the originator of Buffalo Wings. According to news reports, many Buffalonians, in a blind test of the two wing makers' products, chose Quaker Steak and Lube wings over the hometown version. In an average year, the Quaker Steak and Lube turns out eighteen million wings!

One thing that also sets these wings apart is that they come in a wide variety of flavors. Everything from golden garlic to a super, super hot version called Atomic Wings. Patrons must sign a release form before they can be served the hot wings. When it comes to decor, the restaurant hasn't forgotten its roots. The door handles are nozzles from old gas pumps, and a car lift still occupies part of the dining room, holding a 1937 Chevy that sits above the diners. In fact, the three-restaurant complex has nearly forty classic cars and motorcycles on display inside and outside the restaurants. It's a fun place to visit and eat. Open for lunch and dinner; carry-out is available.

Quaker Steak and Lube Restaurant ☎ 412-981-7221
110 Cannily Boulevard • Sharon, Pennsylvania 16146
Location: Sharon, Pennsylvania, is directly across the Ohio border from Youngstown, Ohio.
Handicapped access: Yes.

A HOLIDAY GARDEN CENTER DISPLAY

This is one of my favorite stops. Twice a year, the garden center attracts thousands of visitors from three states to this tiny town by transforming part of its complex into an animated holiday display reminiscent of the old department stores on Euclid Avenue in Cleveland. Hundreds of trees and animals come to life for families to enjoy from shortly after Labor Day until Christmas Eve. During the Easter season, a similar display featuring the Easter Bunny and traditional Easter decorations is also set up for their customers' enjoyment. The best part: It's absolutely free. There is no admission fee, no collection boxes for donations, and no pressure to buy anything in the garden center. It's just the Kraynaks' gift to their customers and friends.

Of course, if you want to buy something, they will be glad to sell it to you.

Kraynak's Garden Center   ☎ 412-347-4511
2525 East State Street • Sharon, Pennsylvania 16146
Location: Sharon, Pennsylvania, is just across the Ohio border, near Youngstown.
Handicapped access: Yes.

AVENUE OF FLAGS

During the Iranian hostage crisis, when Americans were held prisoner by Iranian forces, this small community gained nationwide attention for putting up a new American flag for each day that the hostages were held: a sort of red-white-and-blue reminder to the nation that they were still there. The flags numbered 444 by the time the hostages were finally released. This street, which leads to a local cemetery, has become a local landmark and a tourist attraction. The flags still fly today. Admission to the street is free.

Avenue of Flags   ☎ 800-621-6744
2619 East State Street • Hermitage, Pennsylvania 16148
Location: Hermitage is the town just east of Sharon, Pennsylvania.
Handicapped access: Yes.

GONE WITH THE WIND COMES TO LIFE

It's a little disconcerting when you phone this inn and the lady answers the phone, "This is Tara, Melanie speaking." In the movie *Gone with the Wind*, Melanie Wilkes lived at Tara for a time after the Civil War, but management here claims that the presence of a Melanie at the modern-day Tara is just a coincidence—Melanie is really the name of one of their employees. The Pennsylvania Tara has artifacts from the movie housed in an 1854 mansion befitting the name. The inn has twenty-four rooms, all with private baths. It also contains three restaurants, where breakfast, lunch, and dinner are served. Some of the bedrooms have sunken bathtubs and gas fireplaces, and many of them are named after characters in the book and movie.

In its advertisements, management says that the inn is not suitable for children or pets. (They do note that there are kennels nearby for pets.) Trivia: the owners are the Winner family, who created the anti-auto theft device, "The Club." The restaurants are available to non-guests, as are tours by appointment.

Tara, a Country Inn   ☎ 412-962-3535 or 800-762-2803
3665 Valley View Road, Box 475 • Clark, Pennsylvania 16113
Location: Clark is just minutes away from downtown Sharon, Pennsylvania.
Handicapped access: Steps into inn. However, restaurants are accessible.

ONE BIG CANDY STORE

Daffin Candies claims to have the largest candy store in the world. I don't know if that's true, but I don't argue with people who hand me free candy when I walk in the door. In fact, they give a free sample to everyone who walks into the Chocolate World at the entrance to their factory. Here you will find giant turtles, Ferris wheels, and animals of all kinds made from solid chocolate. Tons of chocolate have gone into these sculptures that have become the Daffin trademark. You can also watch them make some of the candy that has made them famous.

Daffin Candies and Factory Tour   ☎ 412-342-2892
496 East State Street • Sharon, Pennsylvania 16146
Location: Sharon, Pennsylvania, is just across the Ohio border, near Youngstown.
Handicapped access: Yes.

PENNSYLVANIA

75 The Seventy-Nine-Cent Dinner

This is perhaps the one story that has drawn more phone calls and letters than any in the last decade. Pechin Cafeteria, in 1997, was still serving a meal consisting of meat, potatoes and gravy, and a vegetable for—are you ready for this—seventy-nine *cents*! That's right, seventy-nine cents. And they have been charging these low prices for over a dozen years. "What's the catch?" you say. There isn't any. In fact, you can buy coffee and donuts for fifteen cents. A hamburger is nineteen cents, and a hot roast-beef sandwich, with mashed potatoes and gravy, is just sixty-nine cents!

Pechin Cafeteria is part of a larger complex of stores operated by a single family in a depressed area southeast of Pittsburgh. The complex is made up of a large grocery store, a farm and home store, and several other shops. The cafeteria was originally just for Pechin employees, a place where they could get an inexpensive hot meal for less than a dollar. Problem was, there were so many employees that workers in the cafeteria claimed they couldn't always tell who was an employee and who was a customer just taking advantage of an inexpensive lunch. Rather than make an issue of it, the Pechin management decided to just ignore the matter and chalk it up to good public relations. But then the *Wall Street Journal* heard about it and did a story, and that triggered a lot of other national media attention. The end result is that Pechin's is now open to the general public, and the prices are still the same.

How's the food? Well, it tastes pretty much like a meal that costs seventy-nine cents might taste. Seriously, it's not bad, considering the price. Everything is fresh, and the bread is baked on the premises. Lots of local folks come to Pechin's, they claim, not just because of the price, but because the food is good, too. Oh, by the way, if the price is too steep, and you're over sixty-five, try stopping by Pechin's on a Monday. It's free.

Pechin Cafeteria   ☎ 412-277-8602
Pechin Road • Dunbar, Pennsylvania 15431
Location: Dunbar is east of Pennsylvania Route 119 and south of Connellsville, Pa.
Handicapped access: Yes, to restaurant.

A SHORTCUT TO THE STEELERS GAME

For Cleveland Browns fans who may have switched allegiance to the Pittsburgh Steelers, here's a quick way to get to the game when you visit Three Rivers Stadium in Pittsburgh. Go by boat. The Gateway Clipper Fleet is perhaps the largest tour-boat fleet in the United States. One of the services they offer is a boat shuttle to Three Rivers Stadium. This means you don't have to cross the river in your car to get to downtown Pittsburgh. When the game is over, they pick you up by boat and whisk you back across the river, and you are headed for the turnpike while other motorists are still tied up in traffic at the stadium. They also offer a stadium dinner cruise that's a bit more leisurely, giving you a tour of the three rivers and downtown Pittsburgh, and a dinner of hot dogs, fried chicken, baked beans, coleslaw, and other foods connected with a visit to the stadium. Gateway Clipper also offers a variety of other cruises, dinner cruises, and charters.

Gateway Clipper Fleet   ☎ 412-355-7980
Station Square Dock • Pittsburgh, Pennsylvania 15219
Location: Directly across from downtown Pittsburgh, on the Mt. Washington side of the Monongahela River.
Handicapped access: Yes.

A THEME PARK FEATURING MR. ROGERS

This amusement park has been around for a couple of generations. It houses a whole host of entertainment complexes, from Idlewild Park, to Mr. Rogers' Land of Make-Believe, to Story Book Forest—and even offers a circus in the summer. The little kids who grew up with Mr. Rogers on public television will really love this park. In fact, Mr. Rogers loves the park. Fred Rogers, *the* Mr. Rogers, lives not far from here and grew up near Idlewild Park. So it was a natural that this is where he wanted the first and only amusement-park attraction based on his television show. Folks big and little ride the trolley into the land of make-believe and along the way meet all the different characters that are on the show. And, yes, that's the voice of Fred Rogers doing all the parts, just like he does on television. In fact, the park officials say he drops in once in a while just to make sure that they are still doing things his way.

Story Book Forest has been a fixture here for fifty years. It's a gentle spot where the gates are built low for little people. All the nursery-rhyme characters are here, from Humpty-Dumpty to the Old Woman Who Lived in a Shoe, portrayed by humans dressed in nursery-rhyme costumes in combination with larger-than-life sets. For example, kids can climb through the shoe in which the old woman lived, and then sit on her lap and have a story told to them by the daughter of the woman who originated the role fifty years ago.

Idlewild Park　☎ 412-238-3666
U.S. Route 30 • Ligonier, Pennsylvania 15658
Location: On U.S. 30, not far from Ligonier, Pennsylvania.
Handicapped access: Yes.

PENNSYLVANIA

76 That Zippo Lighter Guarantee

We traveled to the town on the bottom of the lighter recently. On the bottom of every Zippo cigarette lighter the words "Bradford, Pa." are stamped. It's here that the famous Zippo guarantee lives on. If you buy one of their lighters and it ever fails to work, or breaks, they will fix it absolutely free, forever.

There are no tours of the plant anymore, but you can visit the Zippo Museum and gift shop. The museum has on display letters from famous Zippo users like General Douglas MacArthur and former president Dwight Eisenhower. They also have mounted some of the damaged lighters that were sent back to be fixed. The oddest one was a pile of metal chips with a short note that the lighter had fallen into a food chopper. (They replaced it, free.) Another was a piece of flattened steel with a letter explaining that the lighter had been run over by a train. (They replaced that one free, too.) You can also see the evolution of the lighter that was born in a small shop above a gasoline station back in the 1920s. They have lighters on display from nearly every year that they have been in business.

Although I am no longer a smoker, I own a Zippo lighter that I picked up while serving with the Marine Corps in the early 1950s. The guide said she was able to tell me the date I bought it from the model number on the bottom of the lighter. I remembered only that it had been purchased sometime in the summer of 1954. Imagine my surprise when she told me that my lighter, which I had brought along to show them, had been manufactured in 1962, eight years after I had purchased it!

The mystery was solved when she questioned me and I admitted that I had broken the top off the lighter, probably in the 1960s, and had sent it in for free repair. Instead of fixing it, they had apparently replaced it with a newer lighter and had engraved my name and serial number, just as they had been engraved on the original, before returning it to me.

By the way, you don't have to be a smoker to carry a lighter today. That's the latest sales pitch that Zippo is using in these days of smoke-free environments. If you have a lighter that you have hung on to for nostalgic reasons, Zippo now makes a new product that will give a new life to your lighter. It's a small flashlight unit that replaces the wheel and flint mechanism inside the lighter. Now when you open your lighter, a beam of light shines out, not a flame. When someone says "Gotta light?" you can say "Yep!" and really give them some light.

Admission to the Zippo Museum is free.

Zippo Museum and Gift Shop   ☎ 814-368-2700
33 Barbour St. • Bradford, Pennsylvania 16701
Location: Bradford, Pennsylvania is southeast of Jamestown, New York.
Handicapped access: Yes.

CLOTHING BARGAIN OUTLET

This is where the clothes that don't sell end up. The Blair Clothing Company has been in the mail-order sales business for nearly a century. If they buy too much, or the merchandise doesn't sell, then it comes to their outlet store here in Erie, Pennsylvania. The bargains, depending on how much you like polyester clothing, can be fantastic. On our last visit, a lady from Parma recognized me and demanded I guess how much the entire outfit she was wearing had cost. It turned out she had bought a shirt, a pair of pants, some socks, and a pair of shoes, and her entire cost was nine dollars and forty-seven cents! Now, I can't guarantee that you would want to wear a blouse that cost fifty cents or a raincoat that costs under twenty dollars, but if you need some inexpensive clothing for whatever reason, this is the place to come.

You never know what will be on sale; trucks from the company headquarters in Warren, Pennsylvania, arrive every day. They usually have all sizes, even extra-large ones for people like me. There are dressing rooms where you can try on the merchandise, but remember this: once you buy it, it's yours. They accept credit cards and are open seven days a week. Another reason for shopping here is that Pennsylvania has no sales tax on clothing, so the price you see on the sticker is the final price you pay. Blair spokespersons claim that you can save up to ninety percent on some of the sale clothing.

Blair Warehouse Outlet   ☎ 814-866-8300
940 Mill Creek Mall • Erie, Pennsylvania 16565
Location: Mill Creek Mall is just north of I-90 in Erie, Pa.
Handicapped access: Yes.

PRESQUE ISLE STATE PARK

One of Pennsylvania's jewels is this peninsula that juts out into Lake Erie and bends back, forming the bay in front of the city of Erie. It provides seven miles of sandy beaches on the lake side and seven miles of picnic areas, boat ramps, and all-people's trail circling the peninsula. There is fishing, swimming, kite-flying, rollerblading, boating, and hiking available, and a multitude of wild animals to watch, like deer and owls. Admission to the park is free and it is open year round. There are no overnight facilities in the park.

Presque Isle State Park   ☎ 814-871-4251
Pennsylvania Route 832 on Presque Isle • Erie, Pennsylvania 16505
Location: Presque Isle is directly across the water from Erie, Pennsylvania, and can be accessed from I-90.
Handicapped access: Yes.

A WATER TAXI TO PRESQUE ISLE

Here's a different way to see one of Lake Erie's finest attractions, Presque Isle State Park in Erie, Pennsylvania. The water taxi is just across from the new waterfront observation tower, so after you see the sights from on high, take a water taxi ride across the bay and do some exploring at the park.

Presque Isle Water Taxi   ☎ 814-455-5892 or 814-866-2830
Erie Public Dock • Erie, Pennsylvania
Location: On the waterfront in Erie, Pennsylvania.
Handicapped access: Steps into boat.

COMMODORE PERRY'S TALL SHIP

This is the tallest "tall ship" on Lake Erie, and a historic one to boot. The *Niagara* was the ship Commodore Perry used in the Battle of Lake Erie when he captured the British fleet during the War of 1812. It has just undergone a four-million-dollar overhaul and has been returned to sailing condition. The ship carries twenty cannons, and its wooden masts soar 100 feet in the air. It has been declared the flagship of Pennsylvania, and spends much of the summer months sailing the Great Lakes visiting other ports. When it is in port, it is open for tours. There is an admission charge. A new birth is being built for it as a part of a multi-million-dollar maritime museum that will soon be located on Erie's lakefront.

U. S. Brig Niagara   ☎ 814-871-4596
Holland Street • Erie, Pennsylvania 16507
Location: On the waterfront at the foot of Holland Street in Erie, Pennsylvania.
Handicapped access: Railings and steps on board ship.

U.S. Brig Niagara. *Courtesy of* U.S. Brig Niagara.

BICENTENNIAL OBSERVATION TOWER

This, the tallest structure in downtown Erie, was built in 1996 as part of the town's 200th anniversary celebration. From atop the tower, on a clear day, you can see Canada. This is also the best spot for an overview of Presque Isle State Park. The tower is 130 feet high. There is a fee for the elevator ride to the top.

Bicentennial Observation Tower   ☎ 814-455-6055
State Street • Erie, Pennsylvania
Location: Dobbins Landing (at the foot of State Street) on the waterfront in downtown Erie, Pennsylvania.
Handicapped access: Yes.

NEW YORK

77 An American Original

Quick, name the one musical instrument that was invented in the United States. Give up? It was the kazoo. Remember the kazoo, that little metal horn you placed in your mouth? Instead of blowing into it, you hummed through it. Well, the company that helped develop the kazoo craze all those years ago is still in business. In fact, it's the only company in America still manufacturing the little metal music maker.

Don't turn up your nose at a kazoo. Musical great Leonard Bernstein used them in one of his orchestra compositions. Recently, factory officials were startled when John F. Kennedy, Jr., dropped in to buy a kazoo. Mr. Rogers, of television fame, has used the kazoo to teach children the fundamentals of music on his television show.

Original American Kazoo.

The factory still uses its 80- to 100-year-old machines to turn out kazoos each day, just as they have for nearly a century. There is a gift shop in front of the factory where you can buy your very own kazoo to take home with you. Factory tours are available during the work day and anytime they might be in the back making kazoos. Just ask.

A small museum in the factory shows the development of the kazoo. You may be asked to sign a petition asking Congress to make the kazoo the official United States musical instrument.

Original American Kazoo ☎ 716-992-3960
8703 South Main Street • Eden, New York 14057
Location: Eden is just south of I-90 west of Buffalo, New York.
Handicapped access: Yes.

WHERE BUFFALO WINGS WERE INVENTED

This bar was the birthplace of an American delicacy: Buffalo Wings. It all started back in the 1960s when a group of regular customers came in very late one night and asked the proprietor for something to eat. They were preparing chicken for the next day's menu, and all that was left was the wings, which in those days were usually used only for soup. However, on this night they quickly cooked up the wings, mixing in some hot sauce that they had made earlier. Fearing that the sauce might be too hot, they cut up some celery and poured out a dish of blue cheese salad dressing to cool burning mouths. From that night on, the word spread. Everyone wanted Buffalo Wings. Today you can get the spicy wings in just about any town in America. But you can also have some in the place where they were created—prepared, it is said, just as they were on that first night over thirty years ago.

Anchor Bar ☎ 716-886-8920
1047 Main Street • Buffalo, New York 14209
Location: In downtown Buffalo, New York.
Handicapped access: Yes, but quite crowded, especially at dinner and lunchtime.

THE BEST BEEF-ON-WECK

If there is one other culinary specialty that western New York is known for, it is the "Beef-on-Weck" sandwich. The origin of this specialty has been argued over for years. For my money, the place that makes them best is Charlie the Butcher's. It is a small cement-block building alongside one of the roads leading to the Buffalo airport.

They take a large steamship round of beef and cook it slowly for twelve hours or more. Then they take a kaiser roll, dust it with some cornflower paste, and sprinkle kosher sea salt on it. They pop it into a hot oven for about five minutes, and the "Weck" roll is ready. Then they slice the beef very thin and pile it up, higher and higher, on the open roll. A spoonful of the beef stock is poured over the beef, and then some homemade horseradish is slathered on the sandwich before it is closed and ready to eat. Excuse me, I have to go get something to eat.

Charlie the Butcher's Kitchen   ☎ 716-633-8330
1065 Wehrle Drive (at Cuayuga) • Buffalo, New York 14221
Location: Wehrle Drive is next to the Buffalo airport.
Handicapped access: Yes.

NEW YORK

78 On the Road to Pollywog Holler

Videographer Ron Strah and I were headed into the forest region of western New York. Bill Castle, who owned a unique bed and breakfast called Pollywog Holler, had given me directions to his place over the phone. As you leave the Seneca Indian reservation on New York Route 17, the towns become smaller and the homes farther apart.

"He said to watch for a barn at the bottom of this hill, on the left-hand side," I told Ron as we started down a long incline with forest on both sides. There at the bottom of the hill was a weathered barn with a gravel road leading off to the left beside it. So far the directions were perfect.

We traveled the gravel road for several miles, noticing that it was getting narrower and rougher. Suddenly, as we crested a small rise in the road, the gravel ended, and stretching out before us was a dirt road that looked as though it had just been freshly carved out of the earth.

"Are you sure this is the right way?" Strah asked me. "This road doesn't look too good, and if it's muddy, we may not get out of here."

"Oh, I'm sure if the road was impassable he would have told us," I replied.

We continued on. The road was passable, but in spots huge holes existed, and boulders that had been unearthed by the grader had to be avoided every once in a while.

We were crawling now, at about ten miles per hour, hoping to see the road resume as a paved highway, or at least a gravel road.

Looking out at the deep forest that surrounded us, I recalled that just that morning I had read a newspaper report that bears had been spotted in this area of New York, and wildlife officials were warning residents to avoid any confrontations with them.

It was at this moment that we crested a hill and even our dirt road stopped. Ahead was just freshly turned earth. It looked like a newly plowed field. It would be impossible to go any farther.

We stopped the car and got out to look around. We walked through the soft dirt, confirming our fears. Had we gone any farther, we would have sunk up to our hubs. Problem was, the carved out dirt road was only as wide as our car, making it impossible to turn around. Backing mile after mile would also be a laborious job because of all the small boulders sticking out of the road that had to be avoided.

I reached for our cellular phone to call Bill Castle and see if he could figure out where we were and offer us some way to get out of our predicament. But we were too far out of a service area for our phone to work. We were stuck.

Ron and I sat there in the car not saying a word, each of us trying to figure out what to do next. I suspect Ron was also thinking a few dark thoughts about the kind of directions I had received. Suddenly Ron said, "Here comes the cavalry!"

Looking behind us I could see a dot on the highway getting larger. Finally the dot turned into a large four-wheel-drive truck. But as it approached us, instead of stopping it just pulled off the edge of the road and prepared to go around us.

We both jumped out of the car and flagged the driver down.

"Is Pollywog Holler around here?" I asked the driver.

"Yup. Just about a mile up the road here," he gestured.

"What about the road?" Ron asked.

"Oh, that," the truck driver answered. "It washed out durin' a big storm about a year ago and since it's not used much, the county has been kinda slow rebuildin' it."

"Well, how do we get out of here?" Ron asked.

"Oh," said the truck driver, as though he just realized we were stuck. "If you want to wait about an hour, I'll get the grader goin' up ahead and come back and cut you a path."

Mumbling to ourselves that we didn't have any choice but to wait, we agreed and watched the driver pull away.

About forty-five minutes later, true to his word, the driver came grinding up the hill in a road grader, pushing small boulders and dirt aside, making a narrow path for us down the hill to where the highway resumed.

Finally on our way again, we had only traveled about a mile when we saw a rusting sign reading "Pollywog Holler." We had arrived. But no one was at the road to meet us. I had explained to Bill Castle that we had a lot of equipment and would need to park as close to his home as possible. He pointed out that his home was a former hunting lodge and was not near the road. In fact, it was a quarter of a mile from the highway on the other side of a woods and stream; the only way to get there was to walk. His last words to me had been "I'll try to work something out."

His solution was sitting beside the driveway. Two large construction wheelbarrows. We decided to carry the equipment in by hand. As Ron unloaded the car, I was looking at the field in front of us. It contained a series of strange sculptures. Some looked like deranged windmills, others like giant tricycles that had been abandoned many years ago. Near the edge of the field was an opening in the woods and a path.

"I don't know where Bill is, but I'll bet that's the path to the cabin," I said as Ron finished putting his equipment in canvas bags for us to carry.

We entered the woods, staggering under our load of cameras, tripods, lights, and other necessary equipment. We had not gone a hundred feet when, rounding a curve, we found a door in the middle of the trail. It was an ornate door, in a doorway, but on either side was nothing. You could just walk around it. Off to the side of the trail we could see what appeared to be mutant mushrooms made of concrete and painted purple. Ahead of us, throughout the woods, were dozens of giant, rusting sculptures, some nearly as big as the trees that sheltered them. Others were tiny objects nearly hidden in the fallen leaves. It was like walking through some strange fantasy land.

It took us about fifteen minutes to reach the other side of the woods, where we could hear the gurgle of a small waterfall. As we approached a wooden bridge, there, on the other side of the stream, nearly hidden in the limbs of surrounding trees, was a huge log cabin and on the porch a smiling, bearded man, waving a welcome. We had finally reached Pollywog Holler.

As we later learned, Bill Castle had once been a businessman, but a heart attack had caused him to change his lifestyle. He went back to school and took art classes and became interested in sculpture. He offered the property around his hunting lodge to colleagues who were also artists as a place to store their projects, hence the variety of work we had seen on the way in from the highway. He had also decided to move out of his modern home and make his hunting lodge into a non-electric bed and breakfast, where he could share his art and his new, healthier lifestyle. A stress-free life was what he was seeking, and it seemed to us that he had found it, as we sat on the huge front porch overlooking a bubbling stream, serenaded by thousands of frogs. Pollywog Holler, he noted, lived up to its name.

Pollywog Holler is equipped with outdoor toilets and has a gravity shower in the sauna. There is natural sparkling water in the well.

Pollywog Holler Bed and Breakfast   ☎ 716-268-5819
R.D. #1 • Belmont, New York 14813
Location: Western New York, in rural area near Belmont. South of New York Route 17 near Olean, New York. Ask for map when making reservations.
Handicapped access: No.

THE GRAND CANYON OF THE EAST

Called the Grand Canyon of the East, this beautiful park stretches for miles through the valley created by the falls of the Genesee River. There are several overlooks where the falls and the valley can be seen. Be careful of deer when driving through the park, especially in the early evening or morning. Brochures on park facilities and maps can be had by writing to park authorities at the following address.

Letchworth State Park   ☎ 716-493-3600
Genesee State Park and Recreation Region
1 Letchworth State Park • Castile, New York 14427-1124
Location: Letchworth State Park is located southwest of Rochester, New York, near U.S. 20A in Castile, N.Y.
Handicapped access: Yes.

GLEN IRIS INN

This was once the home of the Letchworth family. It sits on a ledge overlooking the middle falls of the Genesee River, and is now a very popular inn and restaurant. There are only a few rooms, and reservations are usually needed a year in advance. But call anyway—there are always cancellations. The rooms are modern and have private baths, and the inn is air-conditioned. The view of the falls is worth the year's wait for a room.

Glen Iris Inn   ☎ 716-493-2622
7 Letchworth State Park • Castile, New York 14427
Location: Same as for Letchworth State Park.
Handicapped access: Yes, to some rooms.

FOUR HUNDRED ACRES OF SCULPTURE

More than four hundred acres are covered with fifteen- to twenty-foot—and even taller—surrealistic sculptures. One is of several twelve-foot-tall women running across the top of a farm pond. Much of the art can be seen from the highways near the property, but to really enjoy it, stop in. It is open during good weather. Most of the work is the lifetime achievement of the owner and his students. From high on a hill overlooking one pasture, you might see herds of deer (real ones) wandering among towering sculptures that resemble something out of sci-fi movies.

Griffis Sculpture Park
Ashford Hollow Foundation
67A Mill Valley Road • East Otto, New York 14729
Location: North of the Southern Tier Expressway, State Route 17, near Olean, New York.
Handicapped access: Yes.

A BUFFALO RANCH

This is the largest North American bison ranch in the eastern United States. The herd can be seen from a couple of roads adjoining the property. The owners also have a store, where you can buy fresh bison (buffalo) meat and other bison objects, like horns and skins. Tours of the ranch are offered.

B & B Buffalo Ranch   ☎ 716-699-8813
R.D. #1, Box 154 Horn Hill Road • Ellicottville, New York 14731
Location: Just north of Ellicottville, New York.
Handicapped access: Yes.

B & B Buffalo Ranch. *Courtesy of B & B Buffalo Ranch.*

WEST VIRGINIA

79 Where They Jump off Bridges

When I was a young marine headed for Camp Lejeune, North Carolina, I used to travel through a beautiful part of West Virginia. I always planned my travels so that I could take an hour or so just to stop and gaze at the New River Valley and the area known as Hawk's Nest. This was long before interstate highways and whitewater rafting. It was just a pretty park, with a view that let you see for miles. A couple of years ago I went back to West Virginia and found that a wonderful spot for some family fun had grown up around my favorite rest spot on the way south.

HAWK'S NEST STATE PARK

The park is every bit as beautiful as I remembered it, but now there is a small, thirty-one-room lodge on the mountaintop. Some of the rooms facing the valley have floor-to-ceiling windows, and I booked one on a night when there was a thunderstorm. It was better than television, watching the storm surge up the valley, the lightning spraying light on trees, clouds, and water. There is no extra charge for the rooms with a view, but you do need to get reservations in early, especially in the summertime. The rates during our stay were also quite reasonable, about sixty dollars a night. A restaurant in the lodge offers the same great view of the valley that I had in my room.

Hawk's Nest State Park   ☎ 800-Call WVA or 304-658-5212
P.O. Box 857 · Ansted, West Virginia 25812
Location: South of Charleston, West Virginia, on the New River.
Handicapped access: Yes.

JETBOAT AND TRAM RIDES

There are two great attractions here at Hawk's Nest Park: the jetboat rides down the New River and the tram ride that goes to the bottom of the valley. The fastest and easiest way to get from the top of the mountain to the river in the valley down below is on the tram ride. On this amusement park–style attraction, the cars are fastened to a long cable that snakes its way down the mountain. You sit two on each side and are silently carried down, down, and down. From the top, the river and people look like ants; looking back at the top of the hill as you near the bottom of the ride, it appears as though the lodge is in the clouds.

Once you are on the ground again, head for the boat docks. The Sandstone jetboats traverse the New River daily, except Monday, during June, July, and August. They also run in October when the foliage on the surrounding hills is at its brightest. The ride lasts about forty-five minutes and takes you to the edge of the New River Dam, under several bridges, and to spots where the surrounding mountains form a backdrop for the river. Then it starts upstream, towards the rapids and the New River Bridge. The boat is powerful enough to go through several rapids before it turns around and heads for calmer water. You will get a little wet but do not need to wear any special equipment to ride the jetboat. Reservations are needed, especially during the midst of the summer season. The famous New River Bridge, one of the tallest in the world, is closed one day each year to let parachutists, bungee jumpers, and rappellers climb it and jump to the river below. The Bridge Day Festival attracts thousands of people to the area. This is also where the first whitewater rafting on the East Coast occurred. The original whitewater guides are still in business and will send you and a group on a rubber raft through some of the most thrilling white water in the eastern United States.

Sandstone Jetboats and Tram ☎ 304-469-2525 or 800-Call WVA
Hawk's Nest State Park
P.O. Box 857 • Ansted, West Virginia 25812
Location: South of Charleston, West Virginia.
Handicapped access: Yes to some events, including jetboat rides.

TOUR A REAL COAL MINE

This part of West Virginia is coal-mining country, and the city of Beckley, a surprisingly pretty little town, pays tribute to the miners with tours of this abandoned mine in a city park. The coal mine was used into this century, and real-life miners still go into it every day to check for mine safety hazards. The law treats this just like any working mine. Former and retired coal miners are the guides; they drive the small electric-powered work trains about a quarter of a mile into the earth. Here, in the dim mine lights, you will see how men once worked with shovels and picks to extract the coal. Further into the mine you will also see some of the machines that made mining easier and more productive. The miners will also tell many stories of the cave-ins and poisonous gas that they faced routinely in the old days. Perhaps the most memorable moment of a tour is when the guide asks everyone to sit very still while he turns off the mine lights and the electrical light on his hat. The darkness inside a mine cannot be described. You can put your hand directly in front of your eyes and not see it! Some visitors have been known to suffer instant claustrophobia when the lights go out. Be sure to bring along a sweater; even in midsummer, the temperature inside the mine is a constant 58 degrees. Up on top of the mine, after the tour, you are invited to visit the restored "company town" that includes replicas of the small home where the typical miner and his family lived and of the superintendent's home, which was much larger. There is also a small museum where memorabilia from the mining days is on display. Costumed guides are stationed in each of the buildings to answer questions and talk about the lives of miners.

Nearby is a small children's museum and a pioneer village with log cabins and a one-room schoolhouse.

Beckley Exhibition Coal Mine   ☎ 304-256-1747
New River Park • Beckley, West Virginia 25802
Location: South of Charleston, West Virginia, not far from the Virginia state line.
Handicapped access: Steps into buildings and into mine car.

STATE CAPITOL OF WEST VIRGINIA

The state capitol building here has been listed among the nation's most significant examples of twentieth-century classical architecture. Designed by Cass Gilbert, it is made of buff limestone and has a golden dome that stretches 293 feet into the sky, five feet higher than that of the United States capitol in Washington, D.C.

The building houses 300 rooms and is the keystone to a complex of buildings along the bank of the Kanawha River that includes the state museum, the governor's mansion, and state office buildings. The best time to see the capitol is at night when it is illuminated, and reflected in the nearby river. A statue at the front entrance, *Lincoln*

Walks at Midnight, is a reminder that West Virginia is the only state in the union to have acquired its sovereignty by proclamation of the president of the United States. (Abraham Lincoln proclaimed its statehood in 1863, while the Civil War was raging.)

Tours of the buildings and grounds are available.

State Capitol of West Virginia   ☎ 304-348-3809
Capitol Square
1900 Kanawha Boulevard • Charleston, West Virginia 25305
Location: Off I-64 in downtown Charleston, West Virginia.
Handicapped access: Yes.

West Virginia State Capitol building. *Courtesy of the State of West Virginia.*

SUNRISE MUSEUM

This beautiful museum sits on a hill overlooking downtown Charleston. Here you will find the city's science museum, art museum, and gardens. A pleasant place to spend an afternoon with the kids while exploring the town.

Sunrise Museum   ☎ 304-344-8035
746 Myrtle Road • Charleston, West Virginia
Location: Downtown Charleston.
Handicapped access: Yes.

KENTUCKY

80 Who's Buried in Daniel Boone's Grave?

We had driven to Frankfort, Kentucky, to see for ourselves what the mystery surrounding Daniel Boone's grave was all about. The monument and the tombstone are there, in the Frankfort Cemetery, high on a hill overlooking the Kentucky capitol building. It's a rather simple monument, just an obelisk with carvings on four sides, depicting scenes of Boone's life. He and his wife are buried nearby. But is it really him?

It seems that Boone lived a long life and died, at age ninety, of natural causes, on his son's farm in Missouri. He was buried there in a family plot next to his wife, Rebecca. The year was 1820. However, twenty-five years later, officials in Kentucky started thinking about the man who was the discoverer and first resident of their state, and decided that perhaps Dan should be buried in Kentucky, not Missouri. So they contacted all of his living relatives and got their permission to go dig up the old frontiersman and his wife and bring them back to the Bluegrass State.

When they dug up Daniel, Kentucky officials discovered that all they had was a collection of bones, so they made plaster casts of them and then placed the real bones in a new casket. The funeral was a big one. Reports say the procession from the capitol to the cemetery stretched over a mile. Daniel Boone had officially come home to Kentucky. Or had he?

Someone cleaning out the state historical offices about twenty-five years ago stumbled across the plaster casts made of Boone's bones. There had always been rumors that the Kentuckians were in such a hurry to get Daniel back home that they had dug up the wrong grave. Could it be true? Scientists went to work with the cast of the skull and came up with the conclusion that it was not the skull of a ninety-year-old frontiersman but that of a much younger African-American. It seems that included in the family plot were slaves that once belonged to the family, and it's possible, and even probable, that Daniel Boone's remains are still buried in Missouri.

Despite the scientific evidence, many local folks still insist that Daniel Boone is buried in Frankfort Cemetery.

Daniel Boone's Grave, Frankfort Cemetery   ☎ 502-227-2403
215 East Main Street · Frankfort, Kentucky 40601
Location: In downtown Frankfort, Kentucky.
Handicapped access: Yes.

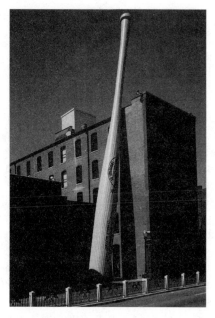

Louisville Slugger headquarters. *Courtesy of Louisville Slugger/John Lair Photography*

WHERE BASEBALL BATS ARE BORN

The Louisville Slugger Baseball Bat Company has come back home to Kentucky. With the opening of its new museum, the company gave up its plant in Jeffersonville, Indiana, across the Ohio River, and came back to the town of its birth.

The new museum has the largest baseball bat in the world standing at the entrance. Inside, after a short film about baseball and the Louisville Sluggers, visitors walk through a full-size dugout and onto the museum's playing field. You'll find several interactive displays here, including one that lets you experience the sensation of a ninety-mile-per-hour pitch coming right at you. The famous memorabilia collection includes bats used by such baseball greats as Babe Ruth and Jackie Robinson. There is even a replica of a white ash forest for you to walk through. (White ash is the wood from which the bats are made.) The big finale is when you walk through the plant itself, where the wood is being turned into bats for professional baseball teams. By the way, each visitor gets to take home a miniature version of the Louisville Slugger, free. The museum is open Monday through Saturday. There is an admission charge.

Louisville Slugger   ☎ 800-282-BATS
800 West Main Street • Louisville, Kentucky 40232
Location: In downtown Louisville, Kentucky.
Handicapped access: Yes.

BEER CAMP

While the Oldenberg Brewery has lost one of its attractions (the world's largest beer and brewing memorabilia collection) its Beer Camp is still a big draw.

Beer Camp is presently held twice a year, in March and September. The 300 slots are usually sold out weeks before the camp begins. Camp consists of a weekend spent immersed in beer culture, including lectures by brewers and beer experts, and taste tests of dozens and dozens of beers from microbreweries and classic brewers from around the world. You will even take a Beer Camp oath and sing the Beer Camp song, which you will be expected to learn. On Saturday afternoon, the campers are taken (by bus) on a pub crawl to some of Cincinnati's more interesting and unusual bars and taverns; or, they can spend the afternoon at Oldenberg Brewery watching and even help make a couple of batches of the Oldenberg brew. They can even spend time, like Laverne and Shirley, on the bottling line.

On Saturday night there is time for a nap before the grand banquet at which a five-course dinner is served, featuring beer in each of the recipes and more beer served to complement each course.

On Sunday there is a commencement ceremony at which T-shirts and diplomas are handed out to the campers. Some people claim it is the proudest moment of their lives.

The cost is $300-plus per person to attend. Remember: only two sessions are held each year, so get your reservations in early.

Oldenberg Beer Camp, Oldenberg Brewery

☎ 606-341-2804 or 800-323-4917
Buttermilk Pike and I-75 • Fort Mitchell, Kentucky 41017
Location: Fort Mitchell, Kentucky, is about ten minutes south of Cincinnati, Ohio.
Handicapped access: Yes to most of the activities at the brewery.

COLONEL SANDERS MUSEUM

The colonel is gone, but not forgotten, at Kentucky Fried Chicken world headquarters in Louisville, Kentucky. His office, just inside the front door, is still the way it was when he was using it. Down the hall is the museum. There is a glassed-in case with lights like those reserved for Tiffany diamonds. Inside sits the blackened cooking pot that Harlan Sanders used to start a chicken empire. You can also see the white suit that he wore on all of his TV commercials. The guide tells us that he chose white so that when he stopped by a restaurant he could fix some chicken, his way, and not worry about spilling flour on his clothes. Displayed are early print ads and awards that were presented to the colonel. By the way, he was never in the military. The title "colonel" was an honorary one given him by the governor of Kentucky. The museum is open Monday through Friday, but is closed on weekends. Admission is free.

Colonel Sanders Museum   ☎ 502-456-8353

1441 Gardiner Lane • Louisville, Kentucky 40232
Location: Near downtown Louisville. Hard to find, get directions by calling first.
Handicapped access: Yes.

THE FIRST CHEESEBURGER

Local legend has it that the cheeseburger was developed here. The owner's father and mother supplied a local school with lunches during the Depression and decided to give the kids a little extra one day by adding a piece of cheese to their daily hamburgers. The results are history. Cheeseburgers became a national food. At least that's the claim here. The cooks at Kaelin's also say that the Golden Arches folks and the rest of the hamburger chains have got the recipe all wrong. Cheeseburgers, they say, should be cooked only in an iron skillet and never, never on a grill. Here, they still make them that way, four at a time in a large iron skillet.

Kaelin's Restaurant   ☎ 502-451-1801
1801 Newburgh Road • Louisville, Kentucky 40232
Location: Several locations around Louisville, but the original, where it all started, is on Newburgh Road in Louisville.
Handicapped access: Yes.

CHRIST'S TOMB IN KENTUCKY

High on a hill in Covington, Kentucky, alongside Interstate 75, stands a replica of the tomb of Christ, overlooking the Ohio River and downtown Cincinnati. The tomb is a life-size copy of the original in Israel. There's also a small garden, chapel, and carpenter shop. The Garden of Hope is operated by a Baptist church in the Covington area and is open for tours, only by appointment and only during spring, summer, and autumn. There is no admission charge, but they do suggest a "love-offering" to help defray the cost of maintenance. The chapel is available for weddings.

The Garden of Hope   ☎ 606-431-3476 or 606-727-8414 or 606-261-2792
Edgecliff Drive • Covington, Kentucky 41011
to raise funds to put in ramps to the tomb.
Location: It can be seen from I-75, just south of downtown Cincinnati.
Handicapped access: Many steps to top of hill where tomb is located.

Christ's Tomb, The Garden of Hope, Covington, KY

ONTARIO, CANADA

81 A Canadian Caper

Let me start by saying that I am second to no one in admiration for the abilities and talents of my colleague and sometime traveling partner, photojournalist Ron Mounts. Down through the years, Ron and his camera have often added much beauty to an otherwise average One Tank Trip. And, when the occasion warrants, he has even risked life and limb to provide just the right video to accompany my words. He has just one problem. Canada.

When the new Windsor gambling casino was about to open in the spring of 1994, Ron accompanied me, my wife, Bonnie, and my son, Craig, across the border to do a story not only on the new casino, but on what else was just across the lake from Cleveland.

Our problems started the first day, when we arrived, only to discover that the construction work, supposedly finished, was still going on, and it was to be another week before the casino would open. And, even though it was spring, that night the city of Windsor was hit with a large ice and snow storm, which played havoc with our plans to set out for Leamington, Ontario, the next day.

We were late and on QE3 (Queen Elizabeth Highway 3) just outside of Windsor. Ron was driving the GMC Suburban we were using on the trip. A string of traffic was ahead of us, and Ron was just keeping up. Suddenly we passed an OPP (Ontario Provincial Police) car, which made a U-turn and started after us. We heard a siren and saw the lights go on on top of the cruiser. Since we were the last car in a line of autos, we assumed he was signaling us to move over so he could take off after a speeder he must have clocked up ahead of us. We, it turned out, were the ones he was after.

A pleasant-faced, gray-haired officer approached our car and asked Ron for his driver's license. Ron asked him what we had done wrong.

"A bit of a hurry, eh?" the patrolman declared. "I clocked you at 118 kilometers."

"I was only going sixty!" Ron protested. "Besides, all those other cars were pulling away from me."

"Looking at the miles per hour instead of kilometers, eh," he said. "Most of you Americans forget that we don't use that system here. Here we use the metric system and the speed limit is 100 kilometers, eh."

"But what about those other cars I saw pulling away from me?" Ron blustered. "They were certainly going faster than I was."

The Canadian officer smiled a Cheshire-cat smile and replied, "But you're the one I stopped, eh?"

He proceeded to write out the ticket and then handed it to Ron with this advice. "If you decide not to pay this, I suggest you not come back to Canada, eh, because this will be in our computers, and if you get stopped for any other offense, I can guarantee you'll be spending some time in Canada as our guest."

Realizing he wasn't going to win this one, Ron accepted the ticket with tight lips, and we slowly pulled back into traffic and crawled on towards our destination with the policeman watching.

But our Canadian adventure wasn't over yet. That evening we were to videotape the Chatham, Ontario, Canadian Legion Bagpipe Band piping down the sun on the rocks at the edge of Lake Erie in Erie Au, a tiny fishing village directly across from Cleveland.

Although it was April, the temperature was in the teens. There was snow on the ground, and a brisk wind was coming off the lake. The pipers were arrayed across large boulders, silhouetted against the setting sun, playing a beautiful rendition of "Amazing Grace." The haunting sound of the pipes was accompanied by swooping gulls, who added their shrill cries to the sound of the bagpipes.

Ron was transfixed by the sight. He dashed around the beach trying to get the best angle of the sun's rays bouncing off the polished pipes, the swinging drumsticks of the drum major, the kilts blowing in the breeze. What he wanted was a shot from the lake that would show the water in the foreground and the pipers on the seawall. There was no other way to do it. Ron had no boots with him, but he waded into the freezing waters of the lake and squatted down, holding his camera, which weighs nearly fifty pounds, just inches above the water. The shot was glorious, it was magnificent! From his cold, wet, uncomfortable position, he caught the last rays of the sun side-lighting the band, their ribbons and kilts blowing in the wind. The pipe major lifted his large silver-topped staff to the heavens, and sunbeams reflected in every direction.

I was watching from a rock, just out of camera range, taking some home video of the scene, and when I saw the pipe major's baton go up, I could almost read Ron Mounts's mind. It was one of those times when you open your mouth to scream a warning, but nothing comes out. I saw everything in slow motion. Ron, spotting the light reflecting from the baton, started to run from the lake towards the rocks. I could see his wet feet slipping in the sand, and as he leaped for a rock to get his camera in closer range, I saw his foot land on the stone, and then slip off. Ron pitched forward, slamming his camera and his chest into the next boulder.

The drums stopped. The bagpipes stopped, with what sounded like the dying scream of an animal. All eyes were riveted on Ron and his camera. I was halfway to him when he climbed to his feet, picked up the camera, and looked through the eyepiece.

"It's okay," he said, motioning the pipers to continue playing. I took a deep breath of relief that Ron was all right, as was his camera. Then I saw Ron's face. It was a study in concentration as he punched and punched the off/on switch on the camera.

Things were not all right, after all.

"I think it's broken," he admitted as we looked at the huge dent in the lens cover on the camera. There were no friendly whirrs or beeps or little lights to signal that it was recording anything. Cleveland, we have a problem.

We were on the other side of the lake, in a foreign country, it was eight o'clock at night, and we still had a day and a half of videotaping to do before we could start home. The nearest television station was over an hour's drive from where we were, and even then, there was no guarantee they could fix whatever had broken in Ron's camera. We had a choice: pack up and go home without our final day's shoot or improvise.

Now, Ron Mounts is a professional, and while he owns one of the little eight-millimeter home-video units, when it comes to his job, he wants to feel the heft of a professional camera, one that uses professional tape and takes pictures that can be shown on TV. What I suggested to him was probably like asking Picasso if he could paint with a broom. I suggested that he take our tiny eight-millimeter home camera and use it to finish up our Canadian shoot. It was as though I had just suggested that he sell his wife and three children into bondage.

However, after he called several TV stations and was told they were unable to help us with our broken camera, the reality of the situation began to sink in, and he reluctantly agreed to try the little camera. He had to tape it to the top of his tripod, and seemed a bit embarrassed each time we would set up in a public place, where people would gather around to see what we were doing. We staggered through the last day of our trip to Canada and were able to use some of the home-video footage in our final product.

About that speeding ticket: Ron vowed not to pay it and never did. His wife, Sandy, fearing that some day they might go to Canada and discover that the Canadian police had long memories, sent the fine in without telling Ron. To my knowledge he has still not been back to Canada.

HILTON INTERNATIONAL WINDSOR HOTEL

This hotel is just a block away from the gambling casino. The rooms facing the Detroit River have a spectacular view from floor-to-ceiling windows that give a 24-hour-a-day panorama of the Detroit skyline. It's especially impressive at night, lying in your bed watching oceangoing ships pass silently up and down the river, while the glow of the skyscrapers across the river lights your room.

Hilton International Windsor Hotel   ☎ 519-253-4411
227 Riverside Drive • Windsor, Ontario, Canada N9A 5K4
Location: Directly across from Detroit, Michigan.
Handicapped access: Yes.

SEE WHAT GROWS IN CANADA

A question. What's farther south: Ruthven, Ontario, or Eureka, California? If you answered Ruthven, you're right. This part of Ontario is known as the Breadbasket of Canada. As the farthest point south in Canada, it has a long growing season, and greenhouses abound. Colasanti's, a part of southern Ontario for generations, is much more than just a greenhouse. It's an art gallery, a restaurant, a desert, a zoo, and a greenhouse all rolled into one. It is a major tourist attraction in this area. There is the grove of orange and grapefruit trees under glass, where a snack bar is located, so even in midwinter you can smell the citrus while enjoying your meal. Some of the largest cacti in Canada are grown here in a man-made desert inside the greenhouse. The zoo houses everything from a buffalo named Cody to rare and exotic birds. There is also a petting zoo for the little kids. Add to this an art gallery and you will see why tour buses roll in every day. By the way, admission is free. Also, if you want to take something back to the states with you, the folks here are very knowledgeable about what you can and can't take through customs.

Colasanti Farms, Ltd.   ☎ 519-326-3287 or 519-322-2301
Route 3 • Ruthven, Ontario, Canada N0P 2G0
Location: Colasanti's and Ruthven are located just inland from Leamington, Ontario, across Lake Erie, from Sandusky, Ohio.
Handicapped access: Yes.

VISITORS' INFORMATION

To obtain more information on this area of Canada, write or call the visitors bureau in Windsor. They will be happy to send you maps and brochures about these and other attractions in the area.

Convention and Visitors Bureau: Windsor, Essex and Pelee Island
☎ 519-255-6530
80 Chatham Street, East • Windsor, Ontario, Canada N9A 2W1
Location: Downtown Windsor, across from Detroit, Michigan.

ACTIVITIES FOR THE WHOLE FAMILY UNDER ONE ROOF

Here are seven acres of fun under one roof. A former canning factory has become a resort that attracts thousands of families year round. Here are some of the amenities: a 250-foot-long indoor water slide, swimming pools, hot tubs, lap pools, racquetball, a bowling alley, tennis courts, a spa for men and women (with beauty services including mudpacks, massage, and nail and hair services), an indoor amusement area with games and bumper cars for the kids, billiard tables, miniature golf, restaurants, fast-food stands, and even rooms for the night. The room rates are reasonable. There are additional charges for the use of some of the facilities, like the spas, bowling, and tennis. One caution: do make reservations as early as possible. As I pointed out, this is a very popular place, with vacationers from both Canada and the U.S., and, especially in the spring, they are sold out very early.

Best Western Wheels Inn   ☎ 519-351-1100
615 Richmond Street • Chatham, Ontario, Canada N7M 5K8
Location: East of Windsor on the 401 Highway.
Handicapped access: Yes.

CANADA BY RAIL

Canada still has a passenger rail service that is a good alternative to airplanes. It is fast, convenient, and runs across the country. We decided to take a One Tank Trip to Canada's capital, Ottawa, by driving from Cleveland to Toronto, leaving our car at the train station, and then taking a four-hour ride east to Ottawa. We found the first-class service comfortable and the food good, and we traveled at an average speed of 98 miles per hour and arrived four minutes early!

Via Rail Service   ☎ 416-366-8411
Location: Train stations are located across Canada, or you may make reservations through Amtrack in the U.S.
Handicapped access: Yes.

CANADA'S CAPITOL HILL

Ottawa is Canada's federal capital, and the beautiful government buildings which contain the House of Commons and the prime minister's offices are open for daily free tours. During the summer months, the governor general's footguards conduct a changing-of-the-guard ceremony each morning on the lawn of the parliament building. The troops are resplendent in their red coats and tall bearskin hats. If you like pomp and ceremony, be sure to catch this attraction. The troops muster each morning at an armory in downtown Ottawa and then march up Elgin Street to the top of Parliament Hill and onto the grounds of the parliament building. Admission to the 45-minute ceremony is also free. The changing of the guard occurs daily from mid-June until August 30th.

Canadian Parliament Building   ☎ 613-996-0896
Parliament Hill · Ottawa, Ontario, Canada K2P 2L7
Location: In downtown Ottawa.
Handicapped access: Yes.

LORD ELGIN HOTEL

This landmark hotel in downtown Ottawa was recently renovated and modernized. It is very convenient to Parliament Hill and
all the downtown shopping, as well as to the Rideau Canal. Also,
troops march past this hotel each morning on their way to Parliament Hill for the changing of the guard. Prices for the hotel are
moderate.

Lord Elgin Hotel   ☎ 613-235-3333 or 800-267-4298
100 Elgin Street · Ottawa, Ontario, Canada K1P 5K8
Location: One block from Parliament Hill.
Handicapped access: Yes.

Canadian Museum of Civilization. *Courtesy of Canadian Museum of Civilization.*

A VERY CIVILIZED MUSEUM

Ottawa is located just across the river from the province of Quebec, and Hull—the city directly across from Ottawa—is home to
one of the major museums of Canada, the massive Museum of Civilization. Here you can trace the human journey through history in

mixed-media exhibits of enormous totem poles, life-size dioramas, cinemax movies, and hands-on activities for children that let them experience many occupations and lifestyles. On Thursdays there is free admission to the museum.

Canadian Museum of Civilization   ☎ 819-776-7000
100 Laurier Street • Hull, Quebec, Canada
Location: Directly across from Parliament Hill, in Hull, Quebec.
Handicapped access: Yes.

AN OLD-WORLD MARKET

This market area in the shadow of the Canadian parliament building stretches for several blocks in all directions. Here you will find both English- and French-speaking farmers selling their produce, cheese, berries, and meats. There are also stands with all types of prepared foods, such as "beavertails," a Canadian delicacy made of fried dough and cinnamon topped with different kinds of jelly. Nearby sidewalk restaurants are a great place to people watch on a sunny day. This is a busy place. Wear a good pair of walking shoes. There are pedicabs available for tours of the market.

Byward Market
Lower Town • Ottawa, Ontario, Canada
Location: In downtown Ottawa, across the Rideau Canal.
Handicapped access: Yes to some buildings.

THE RIDE OF THE MOUNTIES

During the summer months, when the Royal Canadian Mounted Police, or Mounties, are in town and not on tour, they offer their famed musical ride each evening at their headquarters and police college. The Mounties are a symbol of Canada, with their matched black horses and their famed red coats and blue pants with yellow stripes. Admission to the ride is free, but the attraction is so popular that it is usually filled very early. The public is allowed to come out to the stables and parade field on the morning of a ride to watch the rehearsal and inspection. In some ways, this is almost a better attraction than the ride itself. The Mountie band plays while senior officers inspect the men and women and their horses, and then there is a grand procession to the parade field, where a dress rehearsal is held for that evening's performance. For the big finale, forty Mounties line up in two rows and stage an old-fashioned cavalry charge down the field. If you have a chance to see one of their performances, don't miss it.

The Royal Canadian Mounted Police Musical Ride   ☎ 613-993-3571
Canadian Police College, Musical Ride Stables and Practice Grounds
St. Laurent Boulevard, North • Ottawa, Ontario, Canada
Location: On the north side of Ottawa.
Handicapped access: Seats on grass, bring your own chair, paved walkways into barns.

Royal Canadian Mounted Police ride.

CANAL BOAT RIDE

The Rideau Canal was built during the War of 1812, when Canadian forces feared an American invasion of Canada and a canal was dug to provide both a supply route to the capital and an escape route. Today, it is a lovely waterway that wends its way from the capital downtown through the city to a supply lake at the other end. The banks are filled with flowers and side canals. In the winter when the canal freezes over, many people ice-skate to work on the canal, and a winter festival is held here. A glass-topped boat carries tourists along the canal in spring, summer, and autumn.

Paul's Boat Lines   ☎ 613-225-6781
Rideau Canal, across from the National Arts Centre • Ottawa, Ontario, Canada
Location: In central Ottawa.
Handicapped access: Yes.

ONTARIO

82 The Phantom of the Opera

There are more than fifty professional theaters in Toronto, making it one of the major theater centers of the world, and certainly the closest one to northern Ohio. Twenty thousand northern Ohioans travel to Toronto theaters each year. And one play started it all: *Phantom of the Opera*. Now in its eighth year at the Pantages Theater in downtown Toronto, *Phantom* continues to sell out its performances. For those seeking a bargain and wishing to avoid the long drive to Toronto, the company that owns the Pantages Theater offers an ongoing special package that includes motor coach transportation between Northeast Ohio and Toronto, and a room for two for the night in a luxury hotel in downtown Toronto. The trips usually include breakfast or brunch and a stop in Niagara-on-the-Lake, or Niagara Falls, Canada. While dollar values constantly change, this usually is much cheaper than air travel to Toronto, and it takes you right to the door of your hotel and to the theater. There are special savings for groups traveling together. For more information contact the northern Ohio representative of Livent.

Even if you don't belong to a group, there are often a few seats available on charters, and individuals can buy those seats at the group rate. I have been on these tours to Toronto. They are professionally run, and the hotels are usually first class. Regional sales director John Latkovich was formerly employed by the Canadian consul in Cleveland as director of tourism and brings a great deal of experience to his job.

Live Entertainment of Canada, Inc.
☎ 216-942-2420 or (outside 216 area) 800-555-3559
John K. Latkovich, Sales Director
38246 Wilson Avenue • Willoughby, Ohio 44094
Handicapped access: Steps onto bus.

VIRTUAL-REALITY OVERLOAD

You'll love this place if you like cutting-edge, state-of-the-art, virtual-reality electronics. From the moment you walk through the futuristic front door with its lightning-bolt frame, you feel like you've leaped into the future. There are virtual-reality games for just about everything from skiing to hang gliding over the Grand Canyon. You can take part in a realistic race with life-size Indy cars. My favorite was the virtual-reality roller coaster. In an IMAX theater, you sit in a movable chair that shifts, drops, and dips while you watch a point-of-view ride on an incredibly lifelike cartoon roller coaster. You'll find yourself screaming on the hills in spite of the fact that you know it's a movie. Attendants told me they have even had to shut down the movie because some visitors had suffered motion sickness. The way you pay for the rides is also space age. You purchase an electronic card credited with whatever amount you want to spend. Just insert the card in each ride and it automatically deducts the cost of the ride from the card. Also, before you give the card to your children to use, you can have it programmed to refuse access to some games that you don't want them playing. Sega City is open seven days a week.

Sega City   ☎ 905-273-9000
99 Rathburn • Mississauga, Ontario, Canada L5B 4C1
Location: Mississauga is a suburb on the west side of Toronto.
Handicapped access: Yes.

AFTER-THEATER DINING

This is one of the restaurants that Torontonians head to after the theater. Open until 2:00 a.m., the Swiss-style eating place offers a huge variety of food served in an unusual manner. You are given a "passport" as you enter the establishment. The food, from many nations, is prepared and served at small island areas in the restaurant. You take a tray and wander from place to place, picking up sushi here, watching fresh French bread coming out of an oven there, or selecting fish or meat from a butcher who then cooks it for you. At each stop, when you make your choice, the server stamps your passport with the item and the price. When you finish eating, you take the passport to a checkout counter, where it is totaled. The food is quite good and the restaurant is usually busy. No reservations, and there is often a line to get in.

Marche Restaurant
B C E Place Mall
42 Yonge Street • Toronto, Ontario, Canada M5E 1T1
Location: At the foot of Yonge Street in downtown Toronto.
Handicapped access: Yes.

SKYDOME

This is more than a domed baseball stadium: it is also a major entertainment center. The SkyDome is busy almost every day of the year with baseball, football, stage shows, and exhibitions. In fact, the place has become a tourist attraction in its own right. Tours are offered every day that there is no scheduled event. You get to see the press box and some of the loges, and sometimes even get to visit a locker room and go out on the playing field. The SkyDome is the only stadium in the world that has a hotel built into it; it also has several nightclubs and restaurants. A fascinating place. And get this: most of the cost for the project was met by individual corporations. Only a small amount was paid for by taxpayers.

The Toronto SkyDome   ☎ 416-341-2770
Front Street • Toronto, Ontario, Canada M5E 1T1
Location: Downtown Toronto right beneath the CN Tower. You can't miss it.
Handicapped access: Yes.

SkyDome. *Courtesy of SkyDome.*

ONTARIO

83 Smoke and Fire North of the Border

Videographer John "JP" Paustian and I had traveled to Canada to do a series on places to stay north of the border. One of the more delightful stops was at an old gristmill that had been converted into a comfortable inn in the tiny town of Elora, Canada. The town resembled a Scottish village. In fact, it had been built over a century ago by Scottish immigrants to Canada. Low stone masonry walls enclosed some of the homes. Cobblestone streets and sidewalks meandered up and down the rolling terrain, and at the foot of one of them stood the Elora Inn, once the Elora gristmill, built over a small stream. Water rushed in one side of the building, turned a wheel, and then exited the other side to continue its journey downstream. The old mill wheel had been converted to an electric generator and now supplied power, not only for the inn, but for a good part of the town.

The inn had two attractions: its kitchen, where gourmet dishes attracted customers from a hundred miles away, and its rooms.

My room had walls that were two feet thick. The builders of the structure had meant for it to last a long time. The interior of the room had exposed beams and a rustic look.

JP was trying to come up with some way of visually imparting the beauty of the room and its spartan furnishings.

"Why don't you climb into bed," he said, "and I'll turn off the lights. We'll illuminate the room as though moonlight is coming in the window, and we'll hear the sound of the river and see you sleeping."

I agreed, put on a pair of pajamas, and climbed into bed beneath a window with a two-foot-wide sill.

JP put up a stand holding the large television lights in the window well. Then, using a series of shutters, he directed just a small beam of light through a filter onto my face. The effect was just what he had been hoping for. The rest of the light softly lit the room, showing the bare walls and creating a feeling of warmth and great age.

While he set up his camera, I lay in bed idly looking around the barely illuminated room. There, on the ceiling above me, was the nozzle of a sprinkler system for fire protection. Next to it was a round box, apparently a smoke detector, with a small flashing red light. My eyes drifted to the window well where the light stand was situated. The shutters on the light were brand new, and the heat of the big television bulbs was starting to cook off some of the paint. A thin wisp of smoke was drifting up towards the top of the window well and into the bedroom.

"JP," I said, "there's some smoke coming from the 'barn doors' on your light, and there's a smoke detector right above your head. I wonder if . . ."

"Beeeeeeeeeeep!" A shrill scream suddenly came from the smoke detector, causing both JP and I to literally jump.

"The sprinklers!" I shouted. "We've got to shut off the alarm before the sprinklers go off!"

JP leaped into the air and grabbed the shrieking smoke detector with both hands, trying to twist the cover off to get at the battery. Unfortunately, the detector was not the battery type. It was wired into the ceiling, and as he came crashing back to the floor with the cover in his hands, he also brought with him part of the ceiling and the wiring. Pieces of plaster showered down on me in the bed, and we could hear other alarms in the hallway starting to go off.

I grabbed the telephone, trying to reach the front desk to advise them that there was no fire, but the operator cut in, asked me to hang up because the hotel was having an emergency, and hung up on me before I could tell him that we were the cause of the emergency.

"Oh my God, listen to that," JP said. "They must have called the local fire department."

From outside we could hear the low wail of fire engines and other emergency vehicles getting louder and louder.

JP had managed to yank the wires off what was left of the smoke alarm, and the shrill alarm was finally stilled. We could still hear other alarms in the hall and the voices of people coming out of their rooms trying to see what the commotion was all about.

I ran to the window and looked down into the courtyard. Fire trucks were coming across the bridge, and people were running towards the inn.

I dashed back to the phone and again tried the front desk. This time I convinced the operator to not hang up and to listen to me as I explained what had happened.

Within seconds the other alarms in the building were stilled. There was a loud knock at the door. JP answered it to find a gaggle of firemen with axes and a firehose crowding down the hallway.

The fire chief checked the smoke alarm and told inn officials, who had now joined the crowd, that the alarm would have to be checked before the room could be rented again. Then he proceeded to give JP and me a lecture about checking such things as the location of smoke alarms before we created conditions that could be potentially dangerous and cause a panic.

When the firemen left, we turned to the inn manager fully expecting to be told to pack our bags and get out. He looked at us and said, "We'll have maintenance come up and clean things up a bit, eh? Do give us a call first if you decide to set off any more alarms tonight, all right?"

Even the next morning, when we checked out and offered to pay for the damage to the room, the manager displayed real Canadian hospitality and waved off our offer, saying "You boys gave this town the most excitement we've had in the last six months."

Three days later JP and I had another encounter with fire alarms, but this one wasn't very funny.

We had pulled into Toronto and checked into the giant Delta Chelsea Hotel. During the week we had been looking at small bed and breakfasts and quaint inns, and now we wanted to sample the big metropolitan hotels and see what they had to offer. We had a two-bedroom suite with a common entrance on the twenty-second floor of the hotel.

We had just completed an interview with a hotel official in my bedroom, regaling him with the story of our experience at the Elora Inn, and had been reassured that the Delta Chelsea was fireproof, with a good central alarm system.

The hotel spokesperson had only been gone two or three minutes. JP and I were discussing our evening schedule when a klaxon horn went off in the hallway outside our door.

"Well, there goes the fire alarm," JP said, jokingly.

Suddenly a public address speaker in the room came to life. A man's voice, speaking with a heavy foreign accent, said something about an emergency. We could not understand anything else he said.

Just then JP said, "You know, I think I smell smoke."

I sniffed the air and there was an acrid odor coming from the direction of the door to the suite.

The public address system blared to life again with the same man speaking in his heavy accent. This time we understood the words "fire" and "tenth and eleventh floors," and a plea to stay off elevators and stay in our rooms.

Both of us bolted for the door. The hallway outside of our room was filled with heavy black smoke, making it almost impossible to see more than a few feet. To our left was a sign glowing through the smoke that said "Exit."

"I don't know about you," JP said, "but I'm for getting out of here. We can't understand what the emergency is, and it looks more like the fire is on this floor."

I agreed. I pointed to the exit sign and started for it with JP right behind me.

When we opened the door, we were hit in the face with clouds of dark smoke. Coughing and choking, we grabbed the handrail and started down the pitch-black stairwell, feeling our way step by step to the next level down.

We had gone down about three floors when a door above us burst open and a crowd of men and women can running onto the stairs, pushing and shoving, crying and screaming. I was nearly knocked down the stairs, but JP grabbed my arm and pulled me against the wall.

"Let's let them go ahead of us, or we're going to get trampled," he said.

Coughing, I choked out some sort of affirmative answer, but deep inside felt my own panic starting to build. The smoke seemed to be getting thicker, and it was becoming difficult to breathe. Maybe the air would be clearer down near the floor. I started to get on my hands and knees. JP felt me sag and grabbed at my arm again.

"Come on!" he shouted. "If you stop now, the smoke will get you and you'll die!"

Some dim emergency lights flickered on in the stairway, and for the first time I could see the swirling smoke. It was even thicker below us, and it made my eyes sting. I steeled myself, yanked off my jacket, and put it over my head, hoping that by breathing through it I could cut down on some of the smoke I was inhaling.

Still gripping the railing, we felt our way down to the fifteenth floor, where we decided to check the corridor to see if we were anywhere near firemen who might take us off the building with ladders. But before we could reach the door, it flew open and another group of panic-stricken people pushed into the stairway, again nearly trampling us in their haste to get down the stairs and escape the smoke.

The announcement on the public address system was being repeated, and again we could not understand most of it, but we did hear "tenth and eleventh floors."

"Maybe that's where the fire is," I gasped to JP.

"If we can get below those floors, maybe it'll be easier to breathe," he gasped back.

The next few minutes will be forever etched in my memory, a montage of sounds and smells: the sounds of fear as people pushed and shoved by us, the smell of smoke that gagged and choked, and the thought, suddenly occurring, that I might never see my home again.

Suddenly I could feel fresh air!

I whipped my jacket off my head. Below us the stairway was nearly clear of smoke. I looked up and, from a door labeled "10," I could see smoke curling through the cracks. We were just below the floor where the fire was. We were going to make it!

A few minutes later we arrived at the ground floor and pushed through an emergency door into a gray late afternoon in downtown Toronto. Pure, clean air was sucked into our lungs. In front of us, the street was filled with hoses and firefighting equipment. People huddled in blankets. We hustled to the other side of the street and could see smoke pouring from what must have been the tenth and eleventh floors.

We later learned the fire had been set by an arsonist, who was caught when he tried to torch another hotel the next day. Damage was over $100,000 and at least two people had to be taken to the hospital for smoke inhalation.

Talking with fire officials, I learned that we probably would have been safer staying in our rooms, placing wet towels under the door to keep out the smoke, and opening outdoor windows for fresh air. However, they also admitted that they had no equipment that could have extended to the twenty-second floor to rescue us, and that should a rescue have been necessary, we would have had only the choice of trying to reach the roof, where they might have evacuated us with helicopters. Still, they emphasized that the safest thing for us to do would have been to stay in the room and follow instructions.

Since that day I dislike staying above the ninth floor in a hotel.

ELORA COUNTRY INN AND RESTAURANT

This is a lovely getaway that will make you think you are in Europe, not just a few hours north of Cleveland in Canada.

Elora Country Inn and Restaurant   ☎ 519-846-5356
77 Mill Street · Elora, Ontario, Canada N0B 1S0
Location: Northwest of Niagara Falls, near the town of Guelph, Ontario.
Handicapped access: Yes.

THE SHAW FESTIVAL

This is one of the major attractions in Canada. The delightful town of Niagara-on-the-Lake is a great spot for the Shaw Festival, which runs from April until October, with a series of plays and musicals, some written by Shaw and others by his contemporaries. For tickets and information contact the festival office. Ask about packages; sometimes during the early part of the season they have discounted prices for Sundays and midweek. Some of the wonderful hotels in the village offer packages that include theater tickets.

The Shaw Festival   ☎ 416-468-2172
P.O. Box 774 · Niagara-on-the-Lake, Ontario, L0S 1J0
Location: Niagara-on-the-Lake is just about twenty miles east of Niagara Falls, where the Niagara River meets Lake Ontario.
Handicapped access: Yes.

Shaw Festival. *Courtesy of the Shaw Festival.*

QUEEN ELIZABETH SLEPT HERE

This town of 12,000 people has at least a dozen hotels and more than fifty bed and breakfasts—a sign that there's something special going on here. The Pillar and Post is a historic hotel. Queen Elizabeth once chose to stay here during a visit to Canada. The hotel and two other major properties in the village, the Prince of Wales Hotel and the Queen's Landing Hotel, have recently been purchased by a local businesswoman who has invested much money in refurbishing the properties. The Pillar and Post now has an indoor pool and a spa that offers massage, facials, and a host of other services. Some of the rooms offer gas fireplaces, four-poster beds, and whirlpool bathtubs. Each hotel also has several restaurants and bars. One sidelight: When I last stayed there, I noted that on the bill was a "room gratuity" charge. It had been applied without my being told. When I questioned a hotel official, I was told they had decided to add it to all of their customers' bills as an incentive for their employees, and to attract the best help possible. They said that if anyone objected to it, it would be removed from their bill. I have no problem with leaving a tip for the maid, but I think I would like it better if they would at least tell me about the charge when I check out, and then give me the choice of deciding whether to leave a tip and how much it should be.

Pillar and Post Hotel ☎ 905-468-2123 or 800-361-6788
1011 King and John Streets • Niagara-on-the-Lake, Ontario, Canada L0S 1J0
Location: Located on the north side of Niagara-on-the-Lake.
Handicapped access: Yes.

JAMS, JELLIES, AND MARMALADES

Since the 1920s, this little jam-and-jelly shop has been a fixture in the village. The condiments are made from produce and berries raised locally, and there is always a wide selection. The products are shipped all over in the world.

Greaves Jams and Marmalades ☎ 416-468-7831
55 Queen Street • Niagara-on-the-Lake, Ontario, Canada L0S 1J0
Location: On Queen Street.
Handicapped access: Yes.

ONTARIO

84 Timing is Everything

One of the more unusual trips I have taken happened more than twenty years ago when a young Brecksville man announced he was planning to be the first person to fly a hang glider from one country to another. Chuck Slusarczyk said he was going to fly his glider from Edgewater Beach in Cleveland across Lake Erie to Rondeau Bay, Canada, a distance of about fifty-four miles.

The huge kite that he was to dangle beneath had no motor, so to achieve this crossing he had arranged to be towed by a large speedboat that could reach speeds of nearly fifty miles per hour.

"I expect to be in Canada in an hour and a half," Slusarczyk told the reporters who gathered around him on the beach.

It was a beautiful, hot, humid August day, and I had been chosen to cover Slusarczyk's epic flight. Accompanying me were photographers Ralph Tarsitano and John Hamilton. Since TV8 did not have a boat, we had been scrambling to find a speedy craft to keep up with Slusarczyk as he glided above Lake Erie. Our efforts were unsuccessful until then-Cuyahoga County Sheriff Ralph Krieger's men arrived on the scene. They had a sleek cabin cruiser, adorned with the sheriff's star and black-and-white stripes. The boat was equipped with flashing red lights and a crew of three. The deputy sheriff in charge told me that if we didn't mind sharing space with TV5's Lee Bailey and cameraman Tom Polk, we were welcome to come along on the official escort boat.

At 7:00 a.m. Slusarczyk gave the signal that he was ready to go. His giant Searay boat started north, picking up speed. The cable, about a thousand feet long and coiled on the beach, started snaking into the water. Slusarczyk hoisted his hang glider above him, and as the cable became taut, he took a couple of running steps and it lifted him gently into the air. He soared up above the speedboat that was now picking up more speed.

I was on board the sheriff's boat, docked just offshore where we had filmed the takeoff and departure. Now we urged the sheriff's crew to catch up with Slusarczyk and crew as they disappeared into the morning haze over the lake.

What none of us had considered was that the sheriff's boat had only half the horsepower of Slusarczyk's boat, and with the additional weight of eight people our craft's speed was cut even more. We slogged along, straining to catch a glimpse of either Slusarczyk or his northbound boat.

An hour and a half later we sighted land, and as we got closer to the Canadian shore, we could see Slusarczyk's glider resting in the sand. He had made it, but we had missed the entire flight, other than the takeoff.

As we waded ashore, we were greeted by a large number of vacationing Canadians who had heard about the flight on the early morning news and had come down to the beach to see Slusarczyk arrive. Many of them had brought coolers of beer, soft drinks, and sandwiches, and an impromptu welcoming party was already in progress.

"What happened to you guys?" Slusarczyk asked as he offered us each a beer. "I thought you were going to escort me over here."

We explained that we were unable to keep up with his faster boat and had just blown our chance to cover his history-making flight. Slusarczyk, who was always conscious of public relations, said he was considering making another landing, since many of the Canadians had also reached the beach too late to catch his arrival.

With our encouragement, Slusarczyk hooked up his cable to his boat and took to the sky again, this time heading south. A few minutes later, with our cameras trained on the skies, we could see him turn and head back for us, the glider floating through the sky like some giant bird with a human in its talons. As he closed in on the shore, his boat suddenly made a right-angle turn and raced down the shoreline with Slusarczyk maneuvering his glider down to just a foot off the water as he floated by the cameras, then back to the sky as the boat circled. At the top of the circle, Slusarczyk cut loose from the cable, banked his glider, and made a graceful descent right onto the beach in front of the cameras. The Canadians and the reporters broke out in spontaneous applause. Chuck Slusarczyk had just, officially now, made history.

Following interviews and reactions from our Canadian hosts, we all settled down for a beach-party lunch. Finally, at about 1:00 p.m. our sheriff's crew advised us that if we hoped to make our 6:00 p.m. news broadcast, we had to leave for home now. From some Canadian fisherman they had obtained a compass bearing that would take us right to the middle of the mouth of the Cuyahoga River.

Our trip home had been under way for about thirty minutes when the deputy operating the boat motioned photographer Ralph Tarsitano to join him at the wheel. Tarsitano had mentioned to the deputy that he had spent several years in the coast guard and had been stationed at the Port of Cleveland. The deputy wanted to be spelled at the wheel and asked if Tarsitano would take over for a while and just follow the compass bearing. What Tarsitano had neglected to tell him is that he had very little experience piloting a boat—that most of his coast guard service had been as a photographer.

The lake was still as glass, and Tarsitano kept the nose of the boat pointed south as it droned on towards Cleveland. Many of us fell asleep. Tarsitano, meanwhile, was having difficulty reading the compass, which was sitting on a ledge above the steering wheel. So he picked the compass box up and placed it on the floor between his feet so he could just glance down, now and then, to make sure he was on the right course. What he didn't realize was that the compass was now sitting only inches above the motor, and the vibration apparently caused it to fail and swing to another reading.

He had been at the wheel nearly an hour when the deputy in charge picked up his field glasses and peered towards the horizon, expecting to see land. To his surprise, there was no land, only water. It was at this point he discovered that the compass, now on the floor, was swinging from heading to heading.

He took over the wheel and tried to determine our heading by dead reckoning, but it had grown cloudy, there was no sun to be seen, and the waves were starting to increase. He got on the radio to try to get some kind of heading, only to find that for some unknown reason the radio had stopped functioning. "Not to worry," he announced, "Lake Erie is surrounded by land. If we just keep heading in a straight line we'll find land, identify where we are, and just follow the shoreline home."

For the next thirty minutes we all strained our eyes, looking in every direction for some sign of land ... any land. Wondering what we were going to do when we ran out of gasoline.

"Land, I see land!" shouted Lee Bailey of TV5.

Sure enough, dead ahead, there was a long beach and a few pine trees reaching to the sky. But where were we?

Shortly, we grew close enough to identify more features. Just sandy coastline and a few more pine trees. Could it be an area west of Vermilion? Maybe we were near Mentor Headlands?

The deputy, looking through his binoculars, spotted a man walking on the beach. We drew as close to the shore as we dared and whistled and shouted at the man, who had his back to us. The crashing waves on the shore apparently drowned out our calls. The quick-thinking deputy hit the siren on the boat and then shouted through the loudspeaker: "Ahoy!"

The elderly man, apparently startled, literally jumped into the air as he turned around. He finally came down to the shore and shouted to us, "What do you want?"

The deputy inquired, "Can you tell us which way it is to Cleveland!?"

The man replied, "Eh??"

The deputy shouted back through the loudspeaker, "Which way to Cleveland? We're lost!"

"Whatja say?!" shouted back the old man.

"WE'RE LOST, DAMMIT! WHERE THE HELL ARE WE?!" shouted the deputy.

"Oh," answered the old man, "you're at Point Pelee Park."

We were back in Canada, having gone in a circle.

After determining which way was south, the deputy checked our gas and some charts and determined we had enough gas to reach Kelleys Island, where he could refuel before heading for Cleveland. Bailey and I started talking about renting an airplane at Kelleys Island to take us back to Cleveland so we might still make the 6:00 p.m. news with our story.

The weather was growing worse. The waves were now one to three feet, and it was difficult to keep a steady southern course. It wasn't too long before we were once again lost. We could see fishing boats in the distance and aimed towards one. We pulled alongside. It was a commercial fishing boat with a crew that didn't speak English.

Tarsitano pushed to the rail. "Let me talk to them. I think they're Italian, and I understand some Italian." It turned out the crew was Portuguese and didn't speak Italian. But with pidgin English, and lots of hand waving, we finally communicated that we needed directions to Kelleys Island, and they pointed in a southerly direction.

Twenty minutes after 5:00 p.m. we pulled into the dock at Kelleys Island. Bailey and I and his photographer, Tom Polk, leaped off the boat and ran to the nearest telephone to see if we could rent a plane to fly us to Cleveland. The only one available was a four-seater. That meant that Tarsitano and John Hamilton, my photographers, would have to remain with the boat. Grudgingly, they waved me on, agreeing they would return to Cleveland with the deputies after the boat was refueled, while I flew back to try to get the story ready for our 11:00 p.m. news.

An island taxi carried Bailey, Polk, and me to the airport, where we climbed into the small plane. Moments later we were airborne when, suddenly, the pilot pulled out a map and started searching for Cleveland. "I just moved here from Alabama. This is my first day flying this area, and I've never been to Cleveland," he said.

The three of us almost shouted as we told him to forget the map, keep the plane low enough so that we could see the shoreline, and head east until he found the terminal tower.

A half hour later we touched down at Burke Lakefront Airport. I dashed through the terminal, hailed a taxi, and urged the driver to rush me to our studios on South Marginal Road. I literally ran into the newsroom with my film in hand, thinking of how I was going to write about our adventure, when I was greeted by Assistant News Director Dan Hrvatin, who said, "Don't bother to write anything, we don't have room in the show." It was August 8, 1974, and President Nixon had just announced that he would become the first U.S. president in history to resign the office.

As Chuck Slusarczyk later said of his history-making flight that was virtually ignored, "Timing is everything."

A postscript: As I was unwinding in the newsroom, finally having the first food and drink I had had since noon, the telephone rang. The operator said it was a collect call from Ralph Tarsitano. I accepted the call.

"Zurcher," Tarsitano rasped over the phone, "the boat started taking on water when we hit seven-foot waves just off Cedar Point. So we docked here and don't have any way home. What should we do?"

I suggested that he and Hamilton call a cab and have themselves taken, with their equipment, to Griffing Flying Service near the entrance to Cedar Point and charter a plane, as I did, to complete their journey. I didn't have the heart to tell him the story we had been working on all day wasn't going to run.

Another hour went by. I was still trying to write some kind of a story that might be used within the next day or two about the epic flight, when the phone rang again. It was Tarsitano.

"Zurcher!" he screamed in my ear. "There weren't any cabs! We carried most of our equipment all the way over here and the airport is closed. Do you hear me!? Closed for repairs. You got any other bright ideas?"

I confessed I didn't; it was already 9:30 at night.

"I'll handle this myself!" he screamed at me as he slammed down the phone.

I found out later that, using a company credit card, he had enticed a local Buick dealer to rent them a new station wagon, with which he, Hamilton, and the deputies finally made it back to Cleveland.

Somehow, I don't think either Tarsitano, Hamilton, or I will ever forget the day that Nixon resigned the presidency.

LAKE ERIE PERCH AND WALLEYE SERVED UP RIGHT

If you look at a map and follow a line roughly north across Lake Erie from Cleveland to Canada, you will find Erie Au. It's a tiny fishing village with a wintertime population of about two hundred that swells to several thousand when summer comes and vacationers fill the cottages along the sandy beach. There are few eating places here, but they do have Molly and O.J.'s, and that is good. The owners of the tavern and restaurant also own the fish-processing plant in town and some commercial fishing boats. It should come as no surprise that they offer the freshest Lake Erie perch and walleye in town. They serve it Cajun-style, with lemon pepper; or, for purists, just deep fried to a golden brown. They bring large portions out to the table with hand-cut fries and fresh homemade coleslaw. It's worth the trip across the lake just to have one of their fish dinners.

Molly and O.J.'s Restaurant, Tavern and Motel   ☎ 519-676-8812
875 Mariner's Rd. • Erie Au, Ontario, Canada N0P 1N0
Location: As we said, go to Edgewater State Park in Cleveland and start swimming north.
Handicapped access: Some narrow doorways into restrooms.

ICE WINE

Have you ever had ice wine? It's literally made from frozen grapes, which have a high sugar content that makes for a very sweet (and rather expensive) wine. Ice wine is made and sold at this winery. If you want to order some by mail, use the address below. If you would like to visit the vineyards, they are located near Erie Au, in the town of Cedar Springs. There is a farm market here as well as a tasting room where you can sample some of the several delicious varieties of wine that they make. The winery is open year round.

London Winery, Ltd.   ☎ 519-686-8431
560 Wharncliffe Road, South • London, Ontario, Canada N6J 2N5
Location: Cedar Springs is just a couple of miles west and north of Erie Au, not far from Chatham, Ontario.
Handicapped access: Yes.

THE FERRY FROM SANDUSKY TO ONTARIO

The ferryboats that run from Sandusky, Ohio to Leamington, Ontario, dock here several times each week. The other Canadian destination is Kingville, a few miles to the west. The boats can carry both cars and people. They depart Sandusky in the morning and reach Leamington or Kingville about four hours later. They lay over for a couple of hours and depart for Sandusky about 2:00 p.m., returning in the early evening. The last time I was on board, I discovered they offer only machine coffee, pop, and snack foods, and there was no tour guide narration. On a nice day, it's a quiet four hours to do some reading or watch the horizon; but on stormy days, you can bounce around a bit on the top deck. Remember, you are going into another country, and Canada does require proof of citizenship. You will need your birth certificate or passport. A driver's license or social security card won't do. Unless you are planning to drive back home, or are staying in Canada several days, it is best to leave your car at the dock in Sandusky and use taxis to get around for the couple of hours that you will be in Canada.

Leamington Dock   ☎ 800-661-2220 or 519-724-2115
Erie Street • Leamington, Ontario, Canada
Location: Sandusky, Ohio, is west of Cleveland. Leamington, Canada, and Kingville, Canada, are both located directly across Lake Erie from Sandusky.
Handicapped access: Yes.

PELEE ISLAND

Pelee Island is the largest island in Lake Erie and sits just north of the international boundary between Canada and the United States. The island is very rural in character and attracts large numbers of Ohioans to its many beaches, long country roads, cottages, and wineries. If you are seeking nightlife and lots of activities, this is probably not the island for you. Pelee's charm lies in the quiet of its country lanes and its seeming isolation from both mainlands. One of the big events here is the annual pheasant hunt, for which upland game hunters from both Canada and the U.S. arrive in autumn. You can get maps and information about the island from the township clerk's office. Pelee is also visited every day during the sailing season by the ferryboats from Sandusky, Leamington, and Kingville. The only other access to Pelee is by private boat or airplane.

Pelee Island Township Clerk's Office   ☎ 519-724-2931
Pelee Island, Canada N0R 1M0
Location: In Lake Erie, north of Sandusky Bay.
Handicapped access: Yes.

POSTSCRIPTS

POSTSCRIPTS

Strange Place Names

Have you ever wondered about the name of the place where you live? For the most part, it's usually a simple matter. A town near the water might be called Bay Village. A small community where many farmers live might be christened Farmerstown. How about a place of great charm? Charm would be a nice name. In fact, all the places I have cited exist right here in Ohio.

When I was a youngster out in Lorain County, the intersection of State Routes 113 and 58 in Amherst Township was known as Whiskeyville. In my youth there was nothing located there but a couple of service stations and an old bar, named the Timbers because it was made of logs.

One day at the library, while I was perusing a book on local history, the name "Whiskeyville" jumped out at me. I read on and learned that the crossroads had been given that name by locals because at one time there were no fewer than five taverns grouped around the intersection!

Inspired by the serendipitous find, I armed myself with a modern-day atlas of Ohio and set out on a cross-state trip to discover the origin of several other intriguing place names.

The first one was "Knockemstiff" in Ross County. A stop at the county sheriff's office in Chillicothe assured me that there was such a place, but that little was left of it today; no signs, only a general store and a church. Armed with directions, we set out over the hills and down some gravel roads into the back country of Ross County. Videographer Mark Saksa and I were about an hour into our mission when we realized we were lost. One gravel road looked pretty much like the next. The county was obviously saving money on road signs, or vandals were stealing them. After finding ourselves at the same corner we had passed just minutes before, we both confessed our confusion and started looking for someone to show us the way.

That proved to be a difficult task. In sparsely populated Ross County you can drive for miles down a country lane and never see a house, barn, or person. Eventually, at the crest of a small hill, we spotted a decrepit mobile home clinging to its hillside location at a tilt. At the edge of the property was an old apple tree, and under the tree two men, their arms covered with tattoos, were working on the rusted hulk of an old pickup truck. I should point out that Mark and I were traveling that day in one of our large Ford newscruisers, which have many antennas and, at a glance, resemble a police car. We went whipping into the driveway just as the two men looked up and spotted our car. They both dropped their tools and ran pell-mell for the mobile home.

Puzzled by the situation, we sat in the car, wondering whether we should get out or not. We had heard reports that some of the people who live back in the hills of southern Ohio can be unfriendly to strangers. Suddenly a head popped out of the trailer home.

"What 'joo want?" the head shouted.

"We're lost!" I shouted back.

The head materialized into a short, heavy woman with stringy hair, wearing a threadbare dirty black dress. Barefoot, she marched resolutely towards our car. Reaching Mark's window, she looked at him and said, again, "What 'joo want..."

As she opened her mouth, we could see that she only had one tooth left, and it was right in the front of her mouth. I don't know why, but I couldn't take my eyes off the tooth.

"To tell you the tooth . . . I mean, truth," I spluttered, "we're looking for Knockemstiff, Ohio."

Mark was trying to lean away from the woman, who now had her head almost in the window.

"Why you wanna know?" she demanded, spraying spittle over Mark and giving both of us a whiff of something she must have eaten a few days before.

I quickly told her that we were from a television station and explained what our mission was. It must have satisfied her, because she pulled back out of the car and pointed down the road.

"Hit's right at the bottom of the holler," she said, "but ain't nothin' worth seein' there."

We thanked her and quickly backed out of the driveway. As we peeled off down the road, I looked back to see the two men we had apparently frightened still standing in the shadows inside the mobile home.

At the bottom of the hill we found a crossroads, and the woman was right, there *wasn't* much there. A church, a couple of modest homes, and a cement-block convenience store. But then we saw it: the sign in front of the store, though badly faded and in need of paint, read "Knockemstiff Store."

We whipped into the parking lot, and Mark grabbed his camera and started videotaping the sign and the buildings around the intersection, while I walked into the store.

Only a fly-specked fluorescent light illuminated the interior of the building. Some sad-looking apples and limp oranges filled a counter that also offered bread and a few canned goods. A youngish woman behind the counter looked at me as I walked in, but said nothing. I walked to the counter and introduced myself and explained our mission. I asked if she could do a short interview and perhaps explain the community's strange name.

"I don't like newspaper people," she grumbled.

"I'm on television," I explained.

"Don't like them either," she added. "Now git outta my store."

Outside again, Mark and I were standing by the store sign, trying to decide what to do next when a rusty pickup truck pulled in and parked next to the building. One of the largest humans I have seen unfolded from the front seat, wearing camouflage clothing. Behind his head I could see a gun rack with two rifles in it.

"My wife tells me you don't know the meaning of the word 'git!'" he said.

I hastily assured him that we were just leaving but decided to take one more shot at completing our mission. I explained what we were trying to find and appealed to him to perhaps point us to someone who could help us. I don't know if he just wanted to get rid of us or he was amused by what we were trying to do. The next thing I knew he was inviting me into the store, where he went to a telephone and made a call. A few minutes later I was sitting on a lawn chair in front of another crumbling mobile home, as a longtime resident of the community told me this story:

"Long about a hunderd years ago there was three, four taverns at the intersection, real mean places, and two of them taverns, they was each run by a lady. Well, one night a gambler from down in Portsmouth, Ohio, got into a poker game at one of the ladies' taverns and, wouldn't ya know it, he was cheatin' and the lady caught him at it. She tried to throw him outta her place, but he put up a fight and they rolled out into the middle of the road. Well, the lady across the way who run the other tavern, she saw what was happenin' and she come runnin' and jumped into the fight. All three of 'em was rollin' around on the ground, and the crowd of men was gathered round, cheerin' them on, when one of them shouted 'knockemstiff, ladies, knockemstiff!' And you know, everbody started to laugh, and from then on, the name of the town was Knockemstiff."

KNOCKEMSTIFF, OHIO

Ross County
Don't bother trying to find it. It isn't worth the trouble.

DEVIL TOWN, OHIO

Now this one was a little closer to home and not as hard to find. Devil Town, we learned, was once located just northwest of Wooster, south of the Smithville Road. It's just a local place name that was popular in the 1800s when a tannery was located there. Legend has it that on Saturday night when the workers got paid, it was "Devil Town."

Nothing left to see here. Even many locals had never heard of the name. No signs.

FLY, OHIO

This is a tiny speck on the map (no pun intended), at the end of State Route 800 where it intersects with State Route 7. It sits on the edge of the Ohio River. Local folks say it got its name because the village founders couldn't agree on a name. It was getting late when suddenly a fly landed on the chairman's desk, and he looked up and reportedly said, "Let's call it Fly." And they did.

But that's not the way Dib Harmon, who has run the Fly ferry-boat back and forth across the Ohio between Fly and Sisterville, West Virginia, for thirty years, heard it.

Dib says around the turn of the century liquor salesmen from Marietta used to come up to Fly to take the ferry over to Sisterville. Fly didn't have a name then, but the salesmen always identified it to their customers as "that little speck, no bigger than a fly, where the ferryboat runs." He claims that people just began calling it "Fly" because of those liquor salesmen.

Take the ferry ride across the Ohio. It's a great value and a pleasant way to get to West Virginia. It costs a dollar to drive your car on board. No reservation needed. Just drive down to the edge of the Ohio and flash your headlights; Dib will bring the ferry right over to get you. He might even tell you a few stories on the way over.

PEE PEE, OHIO

No, it's not what you think, but it *is* a strange name for a community. Pee Pee is located right next to Waverly, Ohio, in the southern part of the state. There isn't much there; just a motorcycle shop and a service station, which sells bumper stickers that proclaim "I got gas in Pee Pee, Ohio." And of course, there is the problem of what to call the local residents. "Pee Peeans??"

I noticed a certain reluctance on the part of some residents to acknowledge the name. Their township garage has a very small sign, and none of the community-owned vehicles have any kind of township name painted on the sides. In fact, the only other place I could find the name was on a sign, put up by the state, pointing out Pee Pee Creek. It boggles my mind to think about what the sight of all that running water does to people searching for the community of Pee Pee.

Like I said, it's not what you think. Actually, the name was derived from the town's founder, Major Paul Paine, who carved his initials on a tree along the creek. In time, "P. P." became "Pee Pee."

The folks at the gas station think the name is great and love to capitalize on it, but many of the other folks in the community don't think it's very funny.

POSTSCRIPTS

The Vacation from Hell

I am constantly asked, "Where do you go on your personal vacations?" I usually respond with a grimace and a shudder as I recall my own Vacation from Hell.

It started when we decided to take a family trip to Wyoming to visit my stepbrother, Jim Birrell, and his family. Because my father and stepmother were coming with us, we decided to drive, rather than fly, and see a bit of the country between Ohio and Wyoming.

The trip started nicely. I packed our four-door Cadillac with my wife, Bonnie, our son, Craig (who was about seven years old at the time), my father, Oscar, and my stepmother, Edna. The drive proceeded smoothly until our third day of travel. I was behind the wheel as we entered the state of Nebraska.

A series of billboards proclaiming North Platte as the home of Scout's Rest, Buffalo Bill Cody's ranch, piqued our interest. It was a blazing hot day in the Nebraska flatlands. The local radio station said the temperature was approaching 100 degrees as we pulled into the ranch's parking lot. With the sun high in the sky, I grabbed my prescription sunglasses from the sun visor and tossed my regular glasses onto the dash of the car as we climbed out to start our tour.

We spent a pleasant two hours touring the home and barns of the famous Wild West star. As we returned to the parking lot, I winced as I grabbed the sun-baked door handle to open the car. We all climbed in, and I took off my sunglasses and reached for my regular eyeglasses on the dash. As I sat them across the bridge of my nose, it seemed to me the world had just turned a milky-blue color. I ripped off the glasses. Where there had been two optically ground plastic lenses, there were now two oblong-shaped milky-colored globs of plastic. My glasses had melted in the Nebraska heat!

This was in the days before one-hour eyeglass service in the malls and shopping centers. In fact, at that time there were no malls or shopping centers near North Platte. I had no choice but to put on my prescription sunglasses and wear them for the rest of the trip. It caused some curious glances, especially at night when we would walk into a dimly lit restaurant and Bonnie would have to guide me across the room to my seat.

On our fourth day, after dropping my Dad and Edna off at step-brother Jim's home in Cheyenne, Bonnie, Craig, and I continued to Cody, Wyoming, planning to see the famous Cody rodeo.

The clouds were building that afternoon as we drove to the outdoor arena to buy our tickets for the evening performance. As usual, the place was nearly sold out, and the only tickets still available were the most expensive ones. I handed over eighty dollars for three passes, and we went back to our motel to cool off and check out the motel pool. By the time we got there, the sky had darkened and lightning was painting the horizon with jagged streaks. Instead of swimming, we spent the afternoon huddled in our tiny motel room, listening to the grandmother of all western storms crash and bang around us.

It was hours before the storm subsided and the power, which had failed early in the storm, finally came back on. Although the storm was over, the wind now began to howl. I stepped outside to find the temperature had plummeted and the sun was hidden behind low, fast-moving gray clouds that gave a look of November to the July afternoon.

We drove to the arena, our car rocking back and forth from the wind (which the local radio announcer said was now "gusting at speeds of up to seventy miles per hour"). As I dodged the rolling sagebrush and debris that was windborne in front of me, I turned to Bonnie and said, "Surely they will cancel the rodeo because of the high winds."

I had lost interest in the rodeo, but when we reached the flat area where the rodeo was held, the parking lot was filled with cars and pickup trucks.

We clung to each other as we leaned into the wind, trying to make it to the entrance. A lady with a beehive hairdo was sitting inside a small booth at the gate, taking tickets.

"It's a bit windy, tonight," she offered, as she snatched my tickets and punched them, handing the stubs back to me.

"You mean the rodeo is still on?" I asked incredulously.

"Oh, it's just a bit breezy, Darlin'," she replied. "You should have been here last week when it was really windy."

"I think I would like a refund, or tickets for tomorrow night, when it's less windy," I said.

"Sorry, Darlin'," she answered. "There is no refunds if the rodeo goes on. We've never missed a show, except durin' World War II."

Defeated, we staggered into the stadium. My eyes, behind my dark glasses, were stinging from the flying sand, and we were choking on the clouds of dust that engulfed us. We finally found our seats, open bleachers facing the full fury of the storm lashing across the dusty field that served as the arena.

When the wind would momentarily abate, we could get glimpses of bucking horses, and cowboys flying through the air. But much of the time we were covering our faces to keep from swallowing the windblown dust. The howl of the wind covered much of the noise of cowboys, cattle, and horses. Occasionally, when we could see, it was especially fun watching the steer-roping competition. When the cowboys tried to lasso the steers, their ropes blew back, encircling them and their horses, while the steers merrily chased dust clouds around the arena. The wind began to die down just as the evening mercifully came to an end.

But our problems were not over yet.

A few days later we arrived back in Cheyenne to pick up my father and stepmother for the trip home. We had decided to take the northern route through South Dakota to do some sightseeing. Our first stop was at Mount Rushmore in the Black Hills.

Dad had an artificial leg, so he usually rode in the front seat of the car with me to give himself more leg room. We had just parked at the national monument to our presidents and were getting out of the car. Bonnie, Craig, and Edna were in the back seat. All of us got out of the car except my father, whom we noticed had remained inside.

"What's Oscar waiting for?" Edna asked.

"He must be listening to some music he likes," I replied, noting that through the rear window of the car I could see his head bobbing back and forth.

I decided to hurry him along, because the golf cart and guide we had arranged to drive him and Edna to the viewing area at the memorial had arrived. I walked to the passenger door and noticed that instead of bobbing to the time of the music, he seemed, instead, to be thrashing all over his side of the car.

I opened the car door and was greeted with a fusillade of obscenities! He was shouting something about his hand. Then I saw it. He had apparently grabbed the post between the front and back doors when Edna got out of the car, preparing to use it as a lever to swing himself out of the car. She did not see that he was grasping the column, and she slammed the door, trapping his hand!

Fortunately for him, the car had large rubber gaskets around each door and they had cushioned the blow. We took him to a first-aid station, where it appeared that the fingers were badly bruised, but nothing was broken.

More trouble followed, though.

Late that afternoon, as we continued our journey eastward along Interstate 90, the clouds to the north grew darker and darker. It looked as though a real prairie storm was brewing. My stepmother suggested several times that perhaps we should stop for the day and wait out the weather. I discussed it with my father, who agreed with me that the storm appeared to be far to the north and that we could probably drive around it. But the sky grew more ominous. Soon I had to turn on my headlights. Sagebrush began to roll across the prairie on both sides of the road; clouds of dust at times obliterated the sky. Ahead I could see an overpass and several motorcyclists who were parked there scrambling off their cycles. Suddenly one of them ran to the edge of the road, pointing at my oncoming car and waving his hands in a frantic way. Just then the world turned liquid as a cloudburst smashed down on us. I was wrestling with the wheel while trying to see through the windshield. The wind shifted the rain away from the car for a split second, and I could see an off-ramp to the road. I took it, just as the rain increased its fury.

It was at this second that the rear of our car lifted off the road and then slammed back onto the highway, as if a giant hand had picked us up and then dropped us. I slammed on the brakes and skidded to a stop just short of a brick building. I yelled at everyone to put on their seatbelts; the car was rocking back and forth in the wind, and I feared it might roll over at any minute. Suddenly the interior of the car was filled with broken glass and rain and the roar of the storm—our rear window had been unable to withstand the assault of the wind.

Then, just as suddenly as it had started, the melee was over. The storm abated, and we climbed shakily out of the car to assess the damage. My son, Craig, was bleeding from his finger, but Bonnie, who is a nurse, quickly determined it was only a superficial wound. The building we were parked in front of turned out to be a combination gasoline station and restaurant, so she took Craig inside to put a bandage on his wound. Meanwhile, we looked at our car. Pieces of grit and straw were embedded in the paint. Inside the car, where once there had been trim painted to look like wood, there was now bright silver. The paint had been sandblasted down to the bare metal. Our rear window was gone, as were some hubcaps.

We were in the town of Kimball, South Dakota, population about 150. A tornado had just struck, leaving some cars and vans turned over on the interstate highway. As we drove through the tiny town looking for a Cadillac dealer to replace our windows, we could see the tops of trees gone, chimneys toppled, roofs missing. Power, of course, was out in the town, and I-90 to the east was blocked. We decided to head back to the last town we had passed through to seek assistance there.

The local Cadillac-Chevrolet-Buick-Pontiac-John Deere tractor dealer assured us he could fix up our window . . . as long as we could wait around three or four days while the necessary parts were shipped in by bus from Sioux City.

We decided amongst ourselves that it was time to end this vacation—window or no window, it was time to head home. The local dealer gave us directions to a hardware store, where we bought some heavy clear plastic sheeting and some duct tape, with which we fashioned windows. With plastic flapping in the wind, our mud-spattered car without hubcaps, looking like the Okies of the Great Depression, we limped home. We drew crowds wherever we stopped and had to tell and retell the story about our "Vacation from Hell."

POSTSCRIPTS

The One Tank Trip Cars

Down through the years we have used a variety of vehicles to get to our One Tank destinations. In 1980, when the series started, I used my family car, a 1978 Ford. But we wanted a vehicle that would say "vacation... travel... adventure. ..." So we went to Bill and Bonnie Cutcher of Brownhelm and borrowed their vintage 1948 Chevrolet convertible. For the next couple of years the Chevy was the official mascot on all of our trips. But I determined that we needed a different type of car, something that would really stand out. Bill Cutcher answered my appeal by coming up with a classic 1940 Bantam American roadster. That tiny car immediately caught the attention of my viewers.

Neil Zurcher with BMW Isetta.

For the next several years, the diminutive Bantam and I opened each "One Tank Trip." But there was a problem. Since I did not own the car, I did not feel right in asking to drive it more than a few times each year, when we would spend a day shooting generic scenes of the car that we would then use on each of the trips to give the impression that I drove the Bantam to that spot. Also, everyplace I would go, people would ask, "Where's your little car?" The only solution that I could see was to buy my own vehicle.

A year-long search for the perfect car ended in 1989 when we found a 1959 Nash Metropolitan sitting in a warehouse in North Canton. For the next eight years, whenever possible, I drove my Nash Metropolitan on the stories that we did and also displayed the little car at car shows and other events.

In 1996 we decided it was time I had another "new" car. Something different, something . . . unique. We launched a six-month search and came up with a 1957 BMW Isetta 300. We located the car in a small town near Grand Rapids, Michigan. I bought it sight unseen. The owners, a middle-aged couple, assured me over the telephone that the car was in excellent condition and had been "nearly restored." The only problem was a slight carburetor malfunction. I drove through a rainstorm to pick up the car on the appointed day and arrived to be told, again, that there was a slight problem. The car, which they assured me had been running "like a top" just last night, had developed that carburetor problem they had warned me about, and today it just wouldn't start. Probably just the damp weather, they said.

Now, I am a very trusting person and I believed every word they said. How else could I have handed over a check for the full amount they asked for the car, pushed it onto a trailer, and hauled it through a rainstorm back to Ohio? It was after three weeks of repair work and a couple of mechanics that the truth started to evolve. The car's motor and gasoline tank were loaded with sand, and the car had probably not been driven in months! A month later, friends Kevin Ruic, Scott Ruic, and George Kilburg, and my neighbor, H.B. ("Army") Armstrong (who can usually fix most anything), had all taken a crack at making the Isetta run. A BMW Isetta is a strange little car. It only has one door that opens the entire front of the auto, like a refrigerator door. Its four-speed transmission, located on the left side wall, is upside down! George Kilburg finally put it back together late one night, hit the starter, and in a cloud of smoke, it started. We were overjoyed. It ran! We were scheduled to unveil it the next day at the annual Dick Goddard Woolly Bear Parade in Vermilion. But none of us had ever driven it. We all agreed that since George had gotten the car running, he should have the honor of taking the first drive.

George is a longtime commercial airplane pilot and has also spent many years building and racing small race cars. He is a man who can get into just about any car and drive it like an expert. He proved it by backing the little Isetta out of his garage, turning it around, and roaring off down his darkened driveway towards the front of his house. We saw the headlights turn to the left as he steered onto his front lawn in a large, sweeping circle. He came charging back up the driveway, getting closer and closer to the open garage door without any discernible decrease in speed. Just as he whipped by me into the garage, I heard him scream, "Brakes! There's no brakes!"

As I said earlier, George Kilburg is a man of great experience and, thankfully, quick reflexes. While we turned to watch in horror as the little car zoomed into the garage, George managed to pull the emergency brake, locking up the back wheels, as the car skidded across the concrete of the garage, scattering tools, cans of grease, and nuts and bolts, and came to a stop just inches from a workbench that was bolted to a concrete wall.

The next morning, with a new brake line installed, the car reluctantly started and we loaded it on a trailer, bound for Vermilion. I was met there by members of the Buckeye Mets club with their little cars. We had planned to be one unit in the Woolly Bear parade. I showed off the car by driving it around the parking lot. My wife drove the car, and friends took a turn. Finally it was time to drive to downtown Vermilion to line up for the parade. I led the procession of little cars, all of us drawing smiles from people along the route. Just as we reached the starting point for the parade, the Isetta gave a little cough and stopped dead. It wouldn't start. We had fifteen minutes before the parade kicked off.

Kevin Ruic and his friend Cindy Hofmann appeared at that moment on their way to watch the parade. Kevin stripped off his jacket and, with a few borrowed tools, started taking the motor apart, trying to determine why it wouldn't run. Time was running out, and it quickly became apparent that the car was not going to start. Kevin ran to a nearby motorcycle group and asked to borrow some of their tie-down straps. He tied the end of one strap to the front bumper of the Isetta and motioned my wife, Bonnie, to back the Metropolitan up to the front of the Isetta. He then tied two of the straps together to make a tow rope, lashing the Isetta to the Met. Another friend, Gary Rice, was recruited to steer the Isetta while I stood with my head and upper torso protruding through the sunroof, waving to the crowd. And that is how the Isetta made its debut, towed by its predecessor, the Nash Metropolitan, through the entire Woolly Bear Parade.

In the weeks and months that followed, we did get the Isetta running, and it has been taken along on many of my One Tank Trips. The little Nash Metropolitan was loaned to the Crawford Auto-Aviation Museum of the Western Reserve Historical Society and now sits inside the lobby of the museum, where it is the very first car the visitors see. Folks at the museum tell me that it has been a very popular attraction.

INDEX